EASY-TO-BUILD
BOOKCASES
& CLUTTER CONTROL PROJECTS

18 Practical Solutions to Organize Your Home

From the Editors of *Weekend Woodcrafts* magazine
Rob Joseph and Linda Hendry

An EGW Publishing book—Distributed by Fox Chapel Publishing

Fox Chapel Publishing

1970 Broad Street • East Petersburg, PA 17520
www.FoxChapelPublishing.com

© 2004 by Fox Chapel Publishing Company, Inc.

Easy-to-Build Bookcases and Clutter Control Projects: 18 Practical Solutions to Organize Your Home is a compilation of projects featured in *Weekend Woodcrafts* magazine. The patterns contained herein are copyrighted by the authors. Artists who purchase this book may make up to three photocopies of each pattern for personal use. The patterns themselves, however, are not to be duplicated for resale or distribution under any circumstances. This is a violation of copyright law.

Publisher	Alan Giagnocavo
Editor	Ayleen Stellhorn
Editorial Assistant	Gretchen Bacon
Cover Design	Jon Deck
Layout	Amy Wiggins, AW Designs

ISBN 1–56523–248–8

Library of Congress Control Number: 2004110286

To order your copy of this book,
please send check or money order
for the cover price plus $3.50 shipping to:
Fox Chapel Publishing
Book Orders
1970 Broad St.
East Petersburg, PA 17520

Or visit us on the Web at **www.FoxChapelPublishing.com**

Printed in China
10 9 8 7 6 5 4 3 2 1

Because working with wood and other materials inherently includes the risk of injury and damage, this book cannot guarantee that creating the projects in this book is safe for everyone. For this reason, this book is sold without warranties or guarantees of any kind, expressed or implied, and the publisher and the authors disclaim any liability for any injuries, losses or damages caused in any way by the content of this book or the reader's use of the tools needed to complete the projects presented here. The publisher and the authors urge all woodworkers to thoroughly review each project and to understand the use of all tools before beginning any project.

Contents

Contents

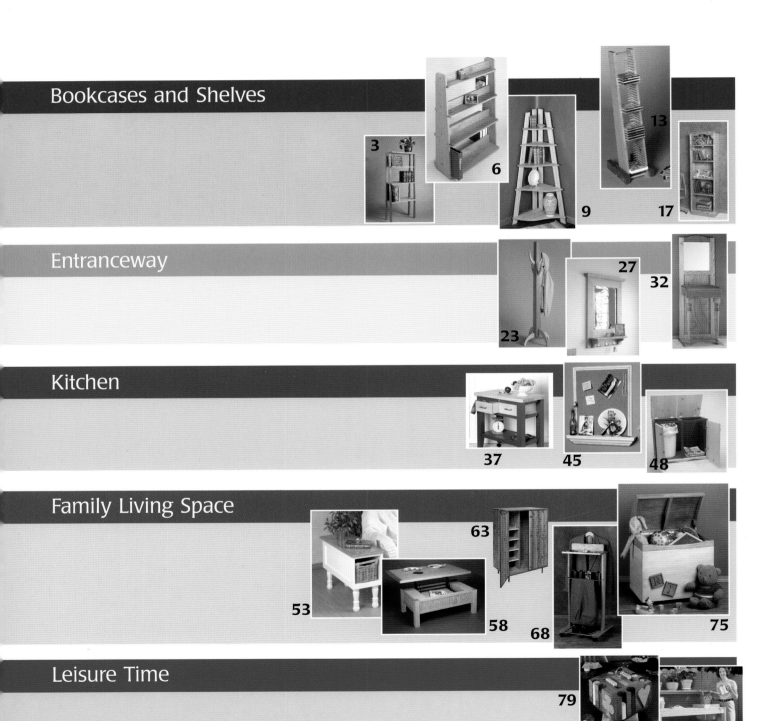

Tools

Table Saw – (Stationary) The 10" table saw is probably the most common and widely used tool in a wood shop. The table saw is mainly used to make straight cuts with the grain, called ripping. It can also be used in a number of ways to make dadoes, rabbets, grooves, and bevels. Crosscuts can be made with the use of a miter gauge.

Circular Saw – (Portable) A circular saw makes straight cuts with the use of a straight edge and saw horses. Nice to have, but they can be heavy.

Drill/Driver – (Portable) A drill/driver is a tool that everyone needs. There are many battery operated models available, along with the corded. These are used to drill holes and to drive screws. Works in the place of the hand-held screwdriver.

Drill Press – (Stationary) The drill press, whether a tall stationary one or the table-top version is a great tool, although not a necessity. It's easier to drill a straight, more accurate hole when using a drill press. Used for drilling, countersinking, mortising (with an attachment), and sanding, with the addition of a drum sanding bit.

Router – (Stationary) The router is a very a useful tool. A router comes separate from the table, but when installed in a router table it is considered a stationary tool. Routers can put those decorative edges on your piece, round over edges, make rabbets, dadoes, grooves, and chamfers. Now, you can even make biscuit slots with the use of the right bit. If you can get a convertible router, one that can go from a standard router to a plunge router, you'll be able to do almost anything.

Plunge Router – (Portable) We show using a portable plunge router for making hanging slots. This can be done with a router table, just plan ahead and make the slot before any curves are cut on the piece. It's much easier to have a straight edge to hold against the fence.

Band Saw – (Stationary) The band saw is used mainly to cut curves. The smaller the width of the blade, the tighter the curve. Band saws can cut thicker wood than a scroll saw or a jigsaw. And with a wide blade installed you can use a band saw to re-saw thicker lumber to get thinner pieces, saving on the cost of lumber.

Scroll Saw – (Stationary) A scroll saw is good for making inside cuts in projects (the band saw cannot do this). It works well on smaller pieces, but is limiting in the thickness of wood used, usually nothing over 1" thick.

Saber Saw – (Portable) The saber saw, also known as a jig saw, is an alternative to use when cutting curves, if the curves are not too small. It's good to use a saber saw on larger projects where using a stationary tool would not be safe.

Finishing Sander – (Portable) Although called a finishing sander, this type of sander can take you through all grits of sandpaper. My favorite is an orbital sander; it fits the hand well, and there's more control.

Biscuit Joiner – (Portable) The biscuit joiner is a great tool for joining wood together. The biscuit joiner cuts a slot. With the addition of a store-bought biscuit and glue, you have a good strong joint along the butted edges of two pieces.

Brad Nailer – (Portable) A brad nailer is fun and fast. Brad nailers come in various sizes, and are either electric or pneumatic (used with an air compressor). Size will depend on your type of projects. But one that can accommodate several sizes of brads is best.

Miter Saw – (Portable) A miter saw is used mainly for cutting angles. They are also used to cut across the grain for wood length. There are several types; a basic miter saw that makes straight cuts and angles, or a compound miter saw where the blade not only pivots, but also tilts.

Miter Box with Saw – (Hand Tool) A miter box is a small table-top tool used with a hand saw that usually comes as a set. As simple as a wooden box with angles cut in it, or a larger one made of metal. A miter box and saw can cut angles, just not as accurately or as fast as a larger miter saw.

Planer – (Stationary) A planer is used to shave down the thickness of the wood. For example, a ¾" stock can be planed to achieve a ½"- ¼" thickness, which gives you much more flexibility when building projects. Re-sawing on a band saw and sanding smooth is an option in some cases.

Supplies

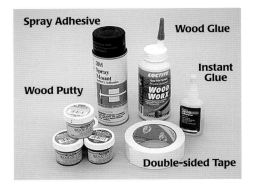

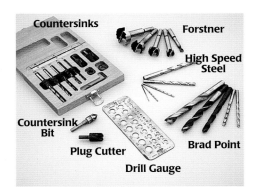

While the power tools are necessary, there are other tools and supplies that are frequently used on all projects. It's a good idea to keep these on hand too:

1. **First-aid kit** – basics, along with eye wash and tweezers.

2. **Fire Extinguisher** – for type ABC fires. (A) wood, trash, and paper, (B) volatile finishing materials, liquid, and grease, (C) electrical equipment

3. **Double-sided Tape** – to adhere patterns or gang wood together before cutting or drilling.

4. **Wood Glue** – sets up faster than white glue. Comes in dark color for darker woods.

5. **Instant Glue** – for wood-on-wood or wood-on-metal adhesion.

6. **Spray Adhesive** – keeps patterns on wood when scroll sawing.

7. **Wood Putty** – fills nail holes before finishing.

8. **Awl** – great for marking hole locations. The mark left from the awl will keep the drill from wandering.

9. **Steel Ruler** – a reliable ruler is a must.

10. **Nail Set** – a tool used to set the nail under the surface of the wood.

11. **Hammer** – a must in any shop.

12. **Chisel and Mallet** – to square or clean up corners after routing.

13. **Square** – keeping things square is important.

14. **Measuring Tape** – easy to keep handy for those longer pieces.

15. **Hack Saw** – needed to cut metal rods.

16. **Glue Brushes** – to spread glue on larger surfaces.

17. **Utility Knife** – good all purpose tool.

18. **Pull saw** – to trim dowels flush.

19. **Clamps** – you can never have enough clamps. Get a variety of sizes and styles (bar, pipe, spring, web).

20. **Wooden Handscrew Clamp** – great for holding small pieces when drilling without marring the wood.

21. **Drill Bit Set** – a good set of drill bits in a variety of sizes. Brad point and forstners are good. A drill gauge helps determine diameters.

22. **Countersink Bit** – used to countersink a hole so the screw head will set under the surface of the wood. A plug cutter to cut plugs for the countersunk holes.

23. **Scissors** – for cutting patterns, tape, etc.

24. **Sandpaper** – 80, 100, 150, 220 grits for a good variety.

Easy-to-Make Bookcase

Laminate

Step 1 - Cut the shelves (A–D) to the dimensions given in the material list. Unless you find stock that is 11½" wide, you will need to laminate two 5¾"-wide boards together per shelf as shown in Step 1. Start with ⅞"-thick stock, then plane the shelves down to their respective thicknesses after they are laminated.

Back Legs

Step 2 - Cut the back legs to the dimensions given in the material list. With a dado head set in the table saw, cut the dadoes that will receive the shelves as dimensioned in the drawing, using the shelves to gauge each dado thickness. (Use the ½" shelf to gauge the ½" dado, the ⅜" shelf to gauge the ⅜" dado, etc.)

Miter Gauge

Step 3 - Use a miter gauge with a sturdy fence as shown in Step 3.

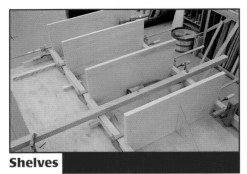

Shelves

Step 4 - On a large work table, glue up the shelves and back legs as shown in Step 4. Use several 1" spacers behind the back legs to achieve a uniform distance of 1" from the back face of each leg to the back edge of each adjacent shelf as dimensioned in the drawing.

Front Legs

Step 5 - Stand the shelf assembly in a doorway so the back legs are perpendicular to the floor. Cut the front legs to the dimensions given in the material list. Mark the distance from the front edge of the top shelf back to where the front leg will be attached as indicated in the drawing. Do the same for the bottom shelf. Line each front leg up along the marked lines and carefully mark the location of the dadoes on each front leg as shown in Step 5.

Cut The Dadoes

Step 6 - Cut each dado on the table saw with a miter gauge set to a 3-degree angle. Make the dado cuts in each leg from either side of the blade as shown in Step 6.

Glue

Step 7 - Glue up the front legs as shown in Step 7.

Cut The Dowels

Step 8 - Cut all of the dowels to the dimensions given in the material list. Make a doweling jig and clamp it firmly to the work when drilling as shown in Step 8.

Material List				**T x W x L**
A	shelf	(ash)	1	½" x 11½" x 23½"
B	shelf	(ash)	1	⅝" x 11½" x 23½"
C	shelf	(ash)	1	¾" x 11½" x 23½"
D	shelf	(ash)	1	⅞" x 11½" x 23½"
E	back legs	(curly maple)	2	1¼" x 2" x 58¾"
F	front legs	(curly maple)	2	1¼" x 1½" x 60"
Supply List				
G	dowel	(walnut)	6	¼" diam. x 1¼"
H	dowel	(walnut)	6	⅜" diam. x 1¼"
I	dowel	(walnut)	6	½" diam. x 1¼"
J	dowel	(walnut)	6	⅝" diam. x 1¼"
K	wood glue			
L	danish oil			

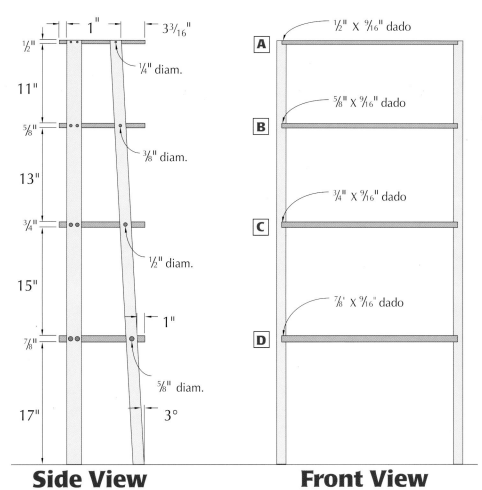

Side View

1" 3³/₁₆"

½"   ¼" diam.

11"

⅝"   ⅜" diam.

13"

¾"   ½" diam.

15"   1"

⅞"   ⅝" diam.

17"   3°

Front View

A   ½" X ⁹/₁₆" dado

B   ⅝" X ⁹/₁₆" dado

C   ¾" X ⁹/₁₆" dado

D   ⅞" X ⁹/₁₆" dado

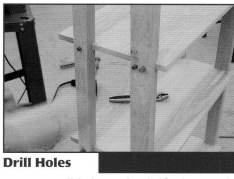

Drill Holes

Step 9 - Drill holes in the shelf sides as indicated in the drawing. Tap dowels into the holes with a dab of glue as shown in Step 9.

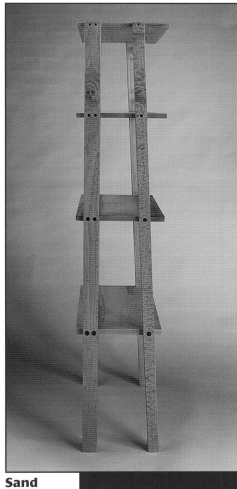

Sand

Step 10 - Sand the entire bookcase assembly through 220-grit sandpaper and apply several coats of oil.

Double-Sided Bookcase

Ripping

Step 1 - We used white oak to make this project, but any stable material will work just fine.

Starting with the sides (A), square one edge with the jointer, then rip the sides to the dimensions given in the material list. Use the table saw to make the ripped cuts as shown in Step 1.

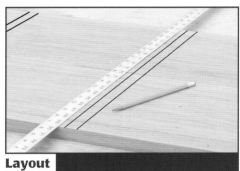

Layout

Step 2 - Dadoes are used to hold the shelving in place. Refer to the drawing on page 8 for the location of each shelf. Lay the sides face side down, butted-up to one another. Use a ruler or straight edge and mark the inside face of each side piece as shown in Step 2.

Cut Dadoes

Step 3 - Make the ¹³⁄₁₆" x ⅜" deep through dadoes using a stacked dado blade on the table saw. Secure the work to a sliding miter table and use a stop block clamped to the fence as shown in Step 3.

Mill the corresponding dadoes in each side piece without adjusting the fence. Repeat this process until all dadoes are milled.

Material List			**T x W x L**
A sides	(white oak)	2	$^{13}/_{16}$" x 10" x 48"
B center dividers	(white oak)	4	$^{13}/_{16}$" x 5" x 30½"
C top shelf	(white oak)	2	$^{13}/_{16}$" x 4" x 31¼"
D upper middle shelf	(white oak)	2	$^{13}/_{16}$" x 5" x 31¼"
E bottom middle shelf	(white oak)	2	$^{13}/_{16}$" x 6" x 31¼"
F bottom shelf	(white oak)	2	$^{13}/_{16}$" x 7" x 31¼"

Supply List			
G oak buttons		24	½" diam.
H wood screws		24	#7 x 1⅛"

Tapers

Step 4 - A slight taper gives the sides a more finished look. Refer to the side view drawing on page 8 for the proper widths at the top and bottom of each side piece. Using a straight edge, draw the taper line down the inside face of each side piece. Use the band saw to cut along the line as shown in Step 4.

Drum Sanding

Step 5 - To clean up any saw marks left behind by the band saw, use the drum sander chucked into the drill press as shown in Step 5.

Exploded View Center Divider

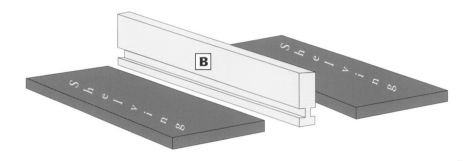

Divider Dadoes

Radius Layout

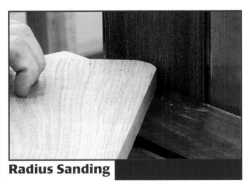

Radius Sanding

Step 6 - Cut the center dividers (B) to the dimensions given in the material list. To help support the shelves, a dado is milled on both sides of the center divider. Refer to the side view drawing for locations of the $^{13}/_{16}$" x $^{3}/_{16}$" deep through dadoes. Use the table saw to mill the dadoes as shown in Step 6.

Step 7 - A slight radius is made at the top of each side piece at the corners. Draw a radius big enough to remove the sharp corners as shown in Step 7.

Step 8 - Use the band saw to knock off the corners, staying just shy of the lines. Smooth the radius using the stationary sander as shown in Step 8.

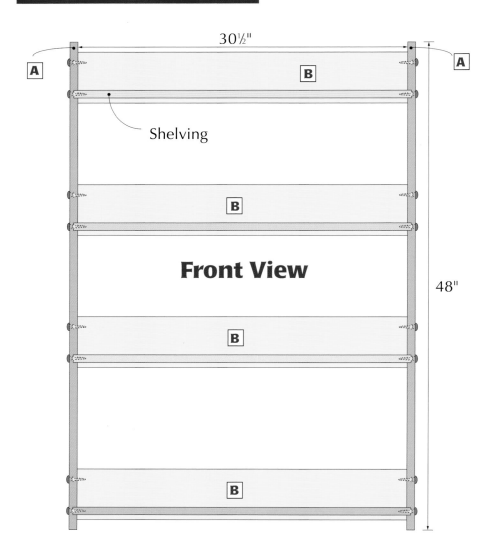

30½"

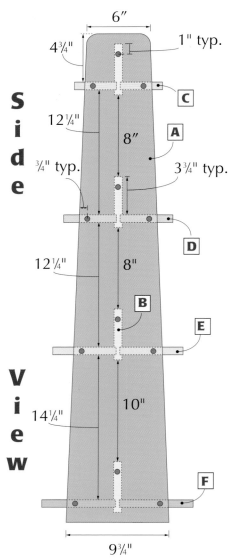

Front View

Shelving

A

B

B

B

B

48"

S i d e **V i e w**

6"

4¾"

1" typ.

C

12¼"

8"

A

¾" typ.

3¾" typ.

D

12¼"

8"

B

E

14¼"

10"

F

9¾"

Side Holes

Step 9 - Pilot holes are needed through the side pieces to accommodate wood screws that will hold the shelves and dividers in place. Refer to the side view drawing on this page for screw hole locations. Mark their locations on the two side pieces as shown in Step 9.

Pre-Drilling

Step 10 - Each hole is countersunk to accommodate a ½" oak button after the screws are inserted into place. Use the drill press to make the countersunk holes in the sides as shown in the inset photo in Step 10.

Cut the shelving (C, D, E, F) to the dimensions given in the material list. Round over all corners that stick out beyond the bookcase. Dry clamp the project together, making sure the shelving is centered. Pre-drill the holes in the side pieces and into the shelving and dividers as shown in Step 10.

Oak Buttons

Step 11 - Use a proper sized drill bit for the #7 x 1⅛" wood screws. Now is a good time to sand the entire project through 220-grit sandpaper.

Put glue into the dadoes on the side pieces. No glue is placed in the dadoes on the center dividers. Clamp and screw the assembly together.

To cover the screws on the sides, insert wooden oak buttons as shown in Step 12.

Finish the piece with several coats of Watco Danish Oil, sanding lightly between each coat, or use the finish of your choice.

Curio Shelving

Cross-Cutting

Step 1 - To achieve the widths required for the shelves in this project, boards are biscuited and butt jointed together. To make the 20" shelf (G), two 11¼" x 20" pieces of oak were glued together. To minimize waste, the off-cut of the 20" shelf will produce the 14" shelf (D).

Cut the widths of the remaining boards slightly wider to allow for jointing the edges in Step 2. The 18" shelf (F) is made from two 9" x 18" oak boards, the 16" shelf (E) is made from two pieces of 8" x 16" boards and the 12" shelf (C) is made from two 6" x 12" boards as shown in Step 1.

Jointing

Step 2 - To get a perfect edge for glue-up, use the jointer on the joining edges of the shelves, as shown in Step 2.

Biscuit Layout

Step 3 - Mate the pieces accordingly. Lay out the biscuit locations across each shelf as shown in Step 3. Be sure not to put any biscuits where any cuts are to be made!

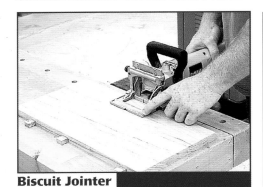

Biscuit Jointer

Step 4 - Use the biscuit joiner or plate joiner set to make slots for the #10 size biscuits (H), as shown in Step 4. Brush glue along the mating edges and into the biscuit slots of each shelf.

Glue-Up

Step 5 - Clamp blanks together, applying pressure until glue begins to squeeze out of the joint, as shown in Step 5. Be sure to label each shelf with a "top edge" location so you remember how the biscuits are located.

Material List				T x W x L
A front side supports	(oak)	2		¾" x 3" x 61"
B back side supports	(oak)	2		¾" x 3" x 61"
C shelf*	(oak)	1		¾" x 12" x 12"
D shelf*	(oak)	1		¾" x 14" x 14"
E shelf*	(oak)	1		¾" x 16" x 16"
F shelf*	(oak)	1		¾" x 18" x 18"
G shelf*	(oak)	1		¾" x 20" x 20"
Supply List				
H biscuits				#10
I buttons		20		½"
J wood screws		20		#6 x 1¼"
K wood glue				
L tracing paper				
M Watco Danish Oil				natural

*See Pattern Packet.

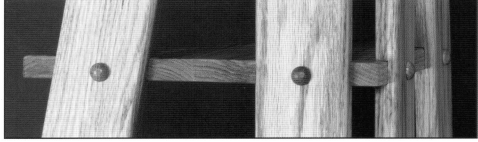

Ripping

Step 6 - Cut the front (A) and back (B) side supports to the widths given in the material list. Use the table saw to make the cuts as shown in Step 6. Cut the lengths to 61".

10° Miters

Step 7 - The two front supports are mitered 10 degrees at their top and bottom edges. Use the miter saw to make the cuts as shown in Step 7.

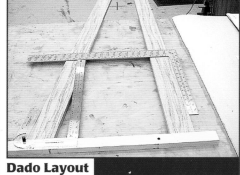

Dado Layout

Step 8 - To assure that the ¾"-wide by ⅜"-deep dadoes on each of the side supports line up, it's a good idea to place their bottom edges against a fixed bottom board that is level. Refer to the side view drawing for the distances between the side supports and the locations of each dado. Using a ruler and square, mark each dado location as shown in Step 8.

Making Dadoes

Step 9 - Use the table saw with a ¾" stacked dado blade raised to a height of ⅜." Use the Dubby® Cutoff Fixture or sliding miter table to run the front supports through the blade with the miter gauge set to 10 degrees as shown in Step 9.

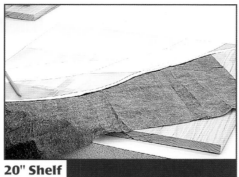

20" Shelf

Step 10 - Repeat these steps for the back supports. Double-check your dado marks before cutting each board by lining them up against each other. Unclamp the shelves once the glue has cured. Tape a copy of the patterns to the top of the 20" shelf. Use tracing paper (L) to trace the pattern onto the blank as shown in Step 10.

Band saw

Step 11 - Use the band saw to make the cut on the shelves, as shown in Step 11. Save the off-cut, for it will be used to make the 14" shelf (D).

14" Shelf

Step 12 - Place the pattern back on top of the off-cut from the 20" piece. Align the pattern's corner in the bottom right portion of the blank. Be sure to follow the grain direction marked on the pattern. Trace the 14" shelf profile onto the blank with tracing paper, as shown in Step 12. Repeat steps 10–11 to make the 12", 16" and 18" shelves.

Drum Sanding

Step 13 - Use the drum sander to smooth cuts and any saw marks left behind from the band saw on each shelf, as shown in Step 13. Be sure to round the corners of each shelf.

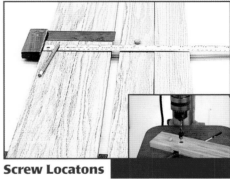

Screw Locatons

Step 14 - A 1¼" wood screw (J) is used to fasten the supports to the shelves. Center each screw on the outside surface on each support. Each screw is located at each dado. Mark the locations for each screw, as shown in Step 14. Countersink each location to a depth deep enough for the ½" buttons (I) to fit into. Use the drill press with a ½" countersinking bit to make each hole, as shown in the Step 14 inset.

Rounding Over

Step 15 - The supports receive a slight round-over along the outside edges. Use the router table and a ¼" bit to knock off the sharp edges as shown in Step 15.

Shelf Rounding Over

Step 16 - Use the same ¼" bit to round over the top edge of each shelf. Only round over the wave portion of the shelf (front edge) as shown in Step 16. Sand all pieces through 220-grit sandpaper.

Assembly

Step 17 - Lay out one side of the supports on the work table. Spread the glue into the dadoes. Hang one end of the supports off the table. Place a shelf into the dado. Pre-drill through the countersunk hole in the supports into each shelf. Screw in place with the wood screws (J) as shown in Step 17.

Button Assembly

Step 18 - Repeat the process until all of the supports are attached to the shelves. Using wood glue (K), place the ½" buttons (I) to hide the screw heads, as shown in Step 18. Finish the project with several coats of Watco Danish Oil, natural (M).

Side View

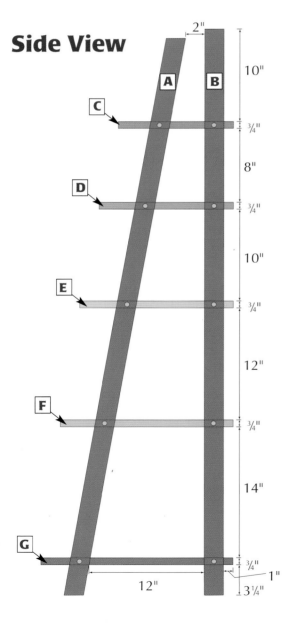

2"

A   B

10"

C   ¾"

8"

D   ¾"

10"

E   ¾"

12"

F   ¾"

14"

G   ¾"
1"
3¼"

12"

Compact Disc

Everyone has extra CDs just lying around the house, so now is a great time to gather them up and put them into their own tower. With the cherry sides and cherry base, this tower will look good in any room of the house.

Ripping

Step 1 - Cut the sides (A) to the width given in the material list. Use the table saw with the fence moved 5" from the blade to make the cuts as shown in Step 1.

Crosscutting

Step 2 - Crosscut the sides (A) to the length given in the material list. Use the radial arm saw to make the cuts as shown in Step 2.

Crosscutting

Step 3 - Refer to the side view drawing on page 16 for the bottom two groove locations on each side blank. Mark the locations on the ends. Use the table saw and miter gauge with a ½" stacked dado blade raised to a height of ¼" to make the through grooves in the bottom portions of each side blank, as shown in Step 3.

Miter Gauge Jig

Step 4 - For the remaining grooves, a simple jig is attached to the miter gauge to ensure proper spacing between each groove. Cut the jig blank (F) to the dimensions given in the material list. Attach the blank to the miter gauge, lining the left side flush with the gauge. Pass the blank through the dado blade. Remove the blank from the gauge and move to the right ³⁄₁₆" and re-attach the blank. Place a ½" piece of scrap into the first groove on the jig blank as shown in Step 4.

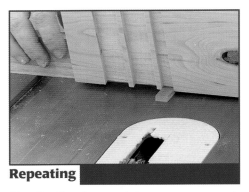

Repeating

Step 5 - Cut the remaining grooves on each side by placing the previous cut onto the ½" scrap blank as shown in Step 5.

Material List

				T x W x L
A	sides	(cherry)	2	³⁄₄" x 5" x 36"
B	base	(cherry)	2	1¼" x 2½" x 11"
C	bottom dowels	(maple)	2	½" x ½" x 8½"
D	top dowels	(maple)	2	³⁄₈" x ³⁄₈" x 6"
E	stopper dowels	(maple)	92	¼" x ¼" x 1¾"
F	miter gauge blank	(scrap)	1	³⁄₄" x 2" x 15"

Supply List

G	wood glue	

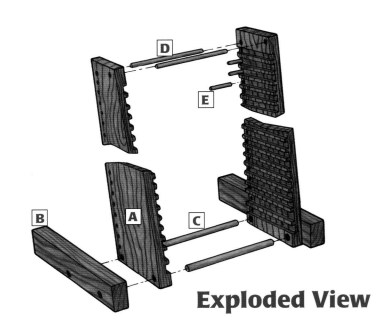

Exploded View

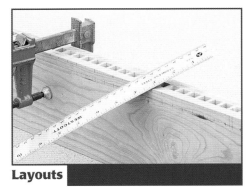

Layouts

Step 6 - Gang the two side blanks together with the insides touching. Refer to the side view drawing on page 16 for stopper dowel locations. Transfer the locations to the sides as shown in Step 6.

Stopper Holes

Step 7 - Use the drill press to drill the ¼" through holes as shown in Step 7.

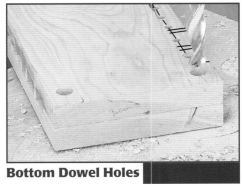

Bottom Dowel Holes

Step 8 - With the sides still ganged together, mark the bottom dowel locations, as shown in the side view drawing on page 16. Use a drill press with a ½" drill bit to make the holes as shown in Step 8.

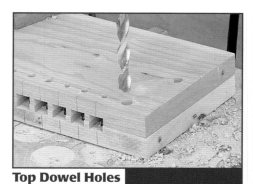

Top Dowel Holes

Step 9 - Mark the top dowel locations from the side view drawing on page 16. Use the drill press with a ⅜" drill bit to make the holes as shown in Step 9.

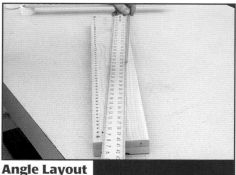

Angle Layout

Step 10 - Measure out from the back edge 3" on the top and make a mark. Measure up from the bottom front edge 4" and make a mark. Using a long straight edge, draw a line from mark to mark as shown in Step 10.

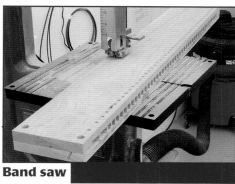

Band saw

Step 11 - Use the band saw to cut the angle from the two ganged blanks, keeping the saw blade just outside the line as shown in Step 11.

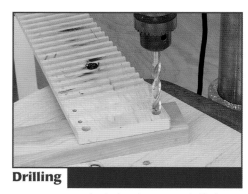

Clean-Up

Step 12 - To clean up the uneven cut left behind by the band saw, use the jointer to remove ¹⁄₃₂" of material as shown in Step 12.

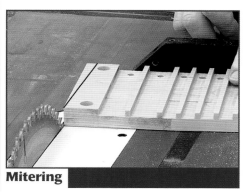

Mitering

Step 13 - Remove the jig from the miter gauge. Rotate the miter gauge 5 degrees to the left of zero. Place the side blank with the groove side up, and the back edge against the miter gauge. Start the cut where the blade hits the front bottom corner as shown in Step 13.

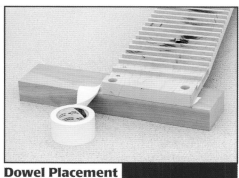

Dowel Placement

Step 14 - Repeat steps for the remaining side. Cut the bases (B) to the dimensions given in the material list. Use double-stick tape and gang the sides to the bases. Place the sides on the bases 1" from the front and flush with the bottom edge as shown in Step 14.

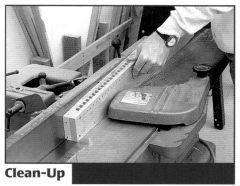

Drilling

Step 15 - Use the holes that were drilled into the sides in Step 7 as guides to drill the ½" through the holes into the bases as shown in Step 15.

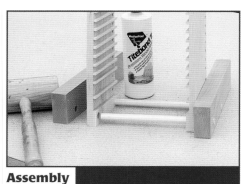

Assembly

Step 16 - Cut the bottom and top dowels (C, D) to the dimensions given in the material list. Refer to the front view drawing on page 16 for proper spacing between each side. Feed the dowel through the top and bottom holes, applying some glue as shown in Step 16. Use a wooden mallet for feeding the dowels through the holes.

Stopper Dowels

Step 17 - Cut the stopper dowels (E) to the dimensions given in the material list. Use the band saw to make the cuts, as shown in the inset in Step 17. Use a dab of glue on each stopper dowel and place them into the holes on the sides until they are flush with the face side of each side blank as shown in Step 17. Sand the entire project through 220-grit sandpaper and finish with several coats of Watco Danish Oil.

Side View
Off Cut

Off Cut

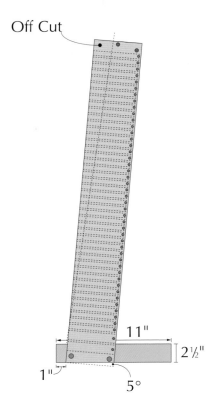

11"

2½"

1"

5°

Side View

3"

3⁄16"

½"

2½"

5⁄8"

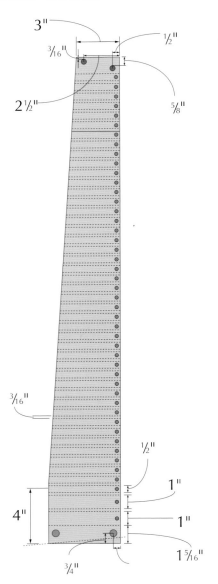

3⁄16"

½"

1"

4"

1"

3⁄4"

1 5⁄16"

Front View

D

½"

35⅛"

E

A

1"

¼"

B

6"

C

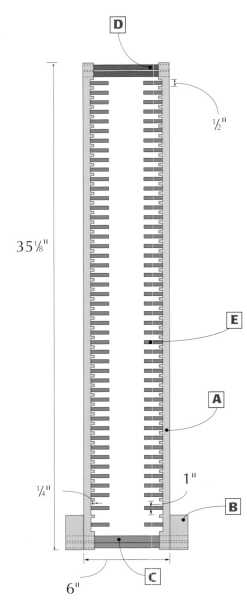

Classic Bookcase

Side Rabbets

Step 1 - Cut the sides (A), top (B), bottom (C), and shelves (D) to the dimensions given in the material list. Refer to the cutting diagram in the pattern packet for the plywood cutting layout.

Step 2 - Use the router in the router table with a rabbeting bit to make a ⅜"-wide by ¼"-deep through rabbet along the inside back edges of the side pieces to allow the back to set in, as shown in the photo above.

Shelf Standard Grooves

Step 3 - To cut the grooves for the shelf standards (P), set up the table saw with a ⅝" dado blade raised to a height of ³⁄₁₆". With the fence 2" from the blade, run a scrap over the dado blades to check the fit. Now make a through groove 2" in from each edge of the sides.

Top Rabbet

Step 4 - To make the rabbet for the top and the dado for the bottom pieces, measure the thickness of the plywood. Ours (and most) are actually ¹¹⁄₁₆". So the dado blades are set to cut a dado ¹¹⁄₁₆"-wide by ⅜"-deep. For the top rabbet, put the fence to the left of the blade with a sacrificial fence clamped and set along the blades (we used the left side of the blade so that we could safely support the side with the table saw's support table). Run a through rabbet across the top inside edge of each side.

Material List				T x W x L
A	sides	(oak plywood)	2	¹¹⁄₁₆" x 11¼" x 72"
B	top	(oak plywood)	1	¹¹⁄₁₆" x 11" x 21¼"
C	bottom	(oak plywood)	1	¹¹⁄₁₆" x 11" x 21¼"
D	shelves	(oak plywood)	4	¹¹⁄₁₆" x 10¼" x 20⅜"
E	back	(oak plywood)	1	¼" x 21¼" x 71⅞"
F	back bottom rail	(oak plywood)	1	¹¹⁄₁₆" x 3⅞" x 20½"
G	top face frame*	(oak)	1	¾" x 6" x 18⅞"
H	bottom face frame	(oak)	1	¾" x 2¼" x 18⅞"
I	side face frames	(oak)	2	¾" x 1½" x 72"
J	shelf banding	(oak)	4	¾" x 1" x 20⅜"
K	base trim*	(oak)	1	¾" x 3" x 19⅝"

Supply List				
L	crown molding		1	1⅝" x 48"
M	wood glue			
N	brads			1", 1¼"
O	biscuits			#0
P	shelf standards		4	72"
Q	shelf brackets and nails		16	
R	Minwax Wood-Sheen			Windsor Oak
S	polyurethane Varathane			Satin

*See Pattern Packet.

Bottom Dado

Step 5 - To cut the dado for the bottom move the fence 4" from the dado blades (keeping the same blade set up as before), and run a through dado along the inside 4" up.

Dry-fit for Back Measurement

Step 6 - Dry-fit the sides, top, and back together using clamps. Square the carcass, and make sure of the measurement for the back.

Step 7 - Cut the back (E) to the dimensions given in the material list or to your dimensions.

Assemble Carcass

Step 8 - Cut the back bottom rail (F) to the dimensions given in the material list.

Step 9 - Assemble the carcass using wood glue (M) and brads (N). Place glue in the top rabbet and bottom dado in the sides. Insert the top and bottom in their respective slots, and brad them in place using the 1" brads at an angle.

Step 10 - Attach the back bottom rail using glue and the 1¼" brads.

Attach the Back

Step 11 - Attach the back by clamping the back in the side rabbets. Make sure the carcass is square. Brad through the back into the sides, top, and bottom rail using the 1" brads.

Face Framing

Step 12 - Cut the top (G), bottom (H), and side face framing (I) to the dimensions given in the material list.

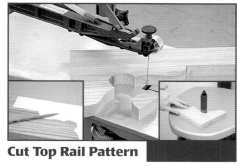

Cut Top Rail Pattern

Step 13 - Locate the top face frame pattern in the pattern packet and trace it to the top face frame, blank flipping the pattern at the center to continue tracing. Cut along the pattern lines using a scroll saw.

Step 14 - Sand the curves using a drum sander, as shown in photo I right inset.

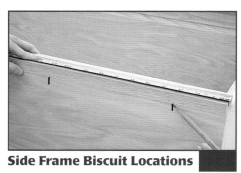

Side Frame Biscuit Locations

Step 15 - Dry-fit the side frames onto the carcass with the bottom edges flush. Clamp together, and mark for biscuits (O) along the sides where the frame meets the sides 3" down from the top and then every 8".

Bottom Frame Biscuit Location

Step 16 - Clamp the bottom frame in place, and mark where the bottom sides meet the side frames for biscuits. Then evenly space five biscuit locations along the top edge of the bottom frame where it meets the front edge of the bottom.

Top Frame Biscuit Locations

Step 17 - Clamp the top face frame in place and mark where the top sides meet the side stiles for biscuits. Then evenly space five biscuit locations along the top edge of the top frame where it meets the front edge of the top piece.

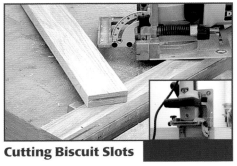

Cutting Biscuit Slots

Step 18 - Cut the biscuit slots in the top, bottom, and side frames. Cut the biscuit slots around the edges of the carcass where previously marked.

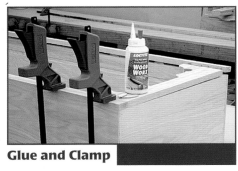

Glue and Clamp

Step 19 - Using wood glue and biscuits, glue and clamp the framing to the carcass. Let dry.

Shelf Banding

Step 20 - Cut the shelf banding (J) to the dimensions given in the material list.

Step 21 - Mark for biscuit slots along the shelf banding and shelf. Make one mark at the center, and make one mark 3" in from each side. Cut the biscuit slots.

Step 22 - Glue and clamp the shelf banding to the shelf. Let dry thoroughly.

Exploded View

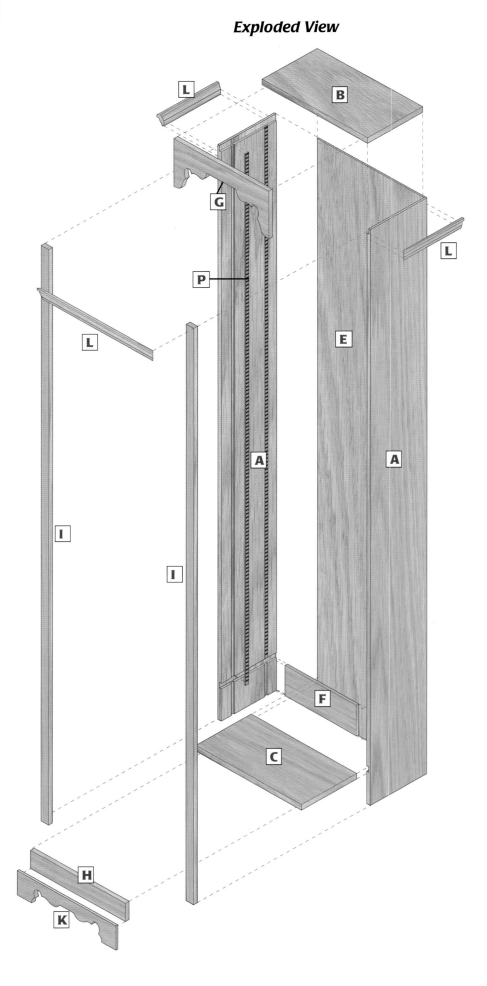

Front View

21⅞"

G

I

E

I

J

H   C

K   F

⅜" rabbet

72"

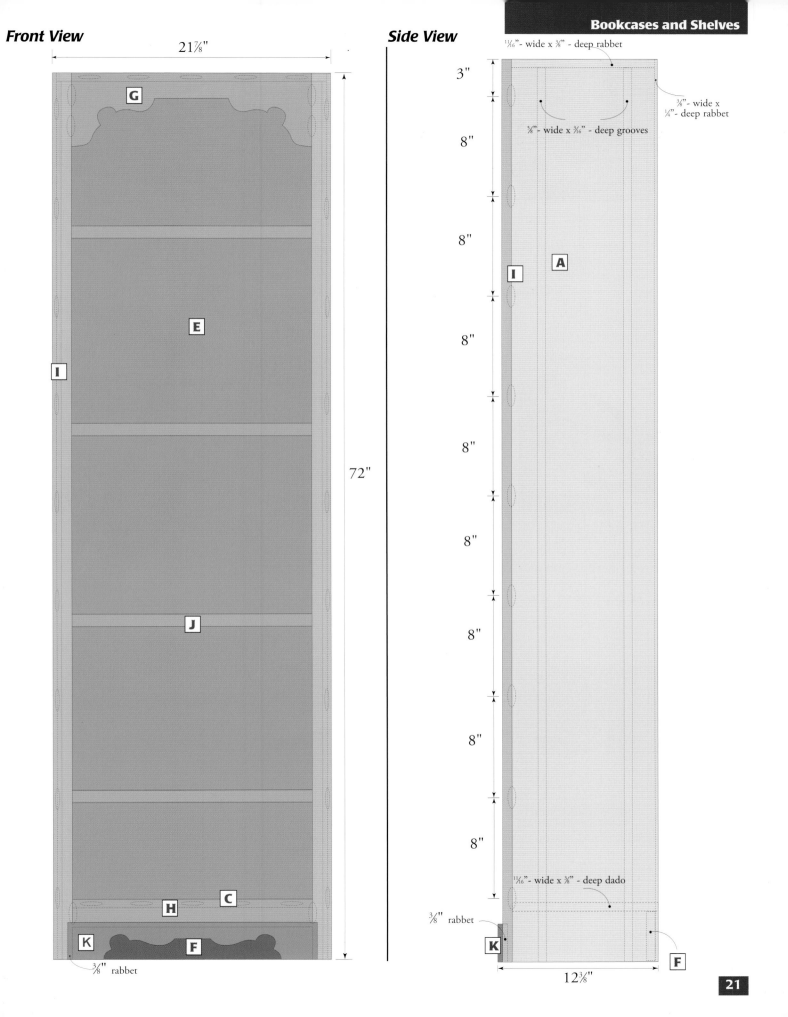

Side View

1¹⁄₁₆"- wide x ⅜" - deep rabbet

⅜"- wide x
¼"- deep rabbet

⅝"- wide x ³⁄₁₆" - deep grooves

3"

8"

8"

I   A

8"

8"

8"

8"

8"

8"

8"

1¹⁄₁₆"- wide x ⅜" - deep dado

⅜" rabbet

K   F

12⅜"

Rout Bottom Trim

Step 23 - Sand the shelves through 220-grit sandpaper.

Step 24 - Cut the base trim piece (K) to the dimensions given in the material list.

Step 25 - Rout a ⅜"-deep by ⅜"-wide rabbet along each end and the top of the base trim piece.

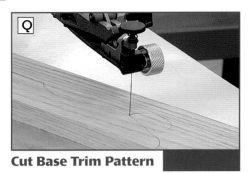

Cut Base Trim Pattern

Step 26 - You can either leave the base trim plain, or you can cut out a design. To cut the design, locate the bottom trim pattern in the pattern packet. Trace along the curves, flipping the pattern in the center. Cut using a scroll saw. Sand the base trim piece.

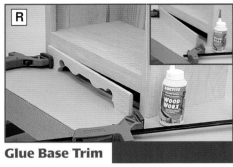

Glue Base Trim

Step 27 - Glue along the rabbet, and clamp the base trim in place. The inset shows the plain trim piece option. Let dry.

Cut Crown Molding

Step 28 - Set the miter saw to 45°, and then measure and cut the crown molding (L) to fit the top of the bookcase.

Step 29 - Set the crown molding flush with the top of the bookcase. Glue in place, and brad, using the 1" brads, as shown in the inset.

Cut Shelf Standards

Step 30 - Cut the shelf standards (P) to 66⅜", using a hack saw.

Step 31 - Finish sand the bookcase and shelves through 220-grit sandpaper and dust thoroughly.

Stain and Varnish

Step 32 - Finish the bookcase and shelves as desired. We used Minwax Wood-Sheen (R), and we followed up with a polyurethane (S). Let dry completely.

Nail in Standard

Step 33 - Using the nails provided with the standards or shelf brackets (Q), nail in the standards.

Place Brackets

Step 34 - Place the brackets where desired, and set the shelves on the brackets.

Coat Rack

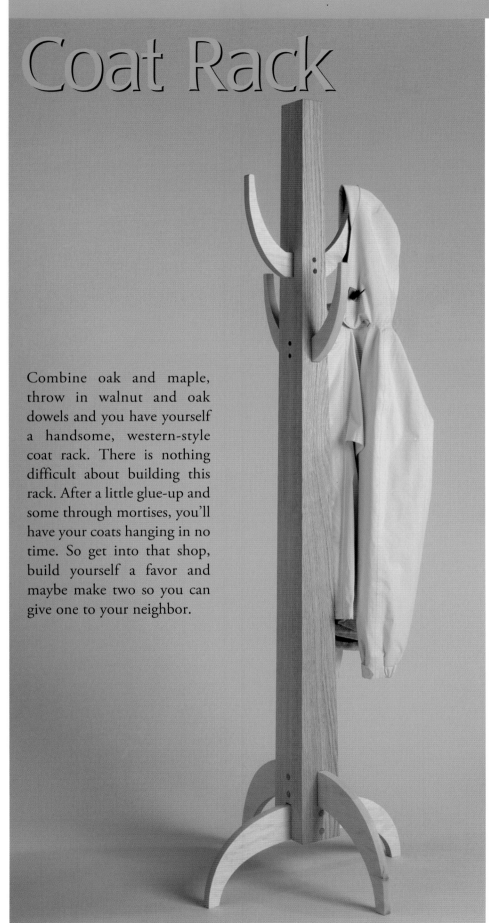

Combine oak and maple, throw in walnut and oak dowels and you have yourself a handsome, western-style coat rack. There is nothing difficult about building this rack. After a little glue-up and some through mortises, you'll have your coats hanging in no time. So get into that shop, build yourself a favor and maybe make two so you can give one to your neighbor.

Body

Step 1 - This oak, maple and walnut coat rack consists of through mortises and through dowels; no mechanical fasteners were used in this project.

To make the body (A) of the coat rack lighter, six $^{13}/_{16}$" x $1^{1}/_{2}$" oak strips are laminated between two $^{13}/_{16}$" x $3^{3}/_{4}$" oak boards. Cut the oak strips and the oak boards to a final length of $61^{7}/_{8}$."

Glue Up

Step 2 - Glue and clamp three oak strips to the bottom $3^{3}/_{4}$" oak board. Set the oak strips edges flush with the edge of the oak board as shown in Step 2. Set aside to dry. Repeat the process for the remaining oak strips. Glue and place the top oak board onto the oak strips. Glue and clamp the entire assembly.

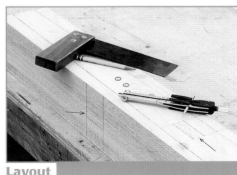

Layout

Step 3 - Lay out the tapers, mortises and dowel locations on the body (A) as shown in the drawings on page 26. Use a square and a compass to lay out the mortise lines and dowel hole locations. Use a long straight edge to lay out the tapers.

Mortise

Step 4 - Make the ¾"-wide x 2"-long through mortises down the center of the body for the top hooks (B) using the drill press and the mortising attachment as shown in Step 4. Make the ¾"-wide x 3"-long through mortises on the bottom of the body for the upper and lower legs using this same method.

Material List				T x W x L
A body	(oak)	1		3¾" x 4" x 61⅞"
B top hooks*	(maple)	2		¾" x 9½" x 11½"
C upper bottom leg*	(maple)	1		¾" x 10½" x 20½"
D lower bottom leg*	(maple)	1		¾" x 7½" x 20½"
Supply List				
E dowels	(walnut)	4		⅜" diam. x 3½"
F dowels	(oak)	4		½" diam. x 4½"

*See Pattern Packet.

Doweling

Step 5 - Dowels are used to hold the top hooks and lower legs in place. Use the drill press with the proper size drill bit to make the through dowel holes as shown in Step 5.

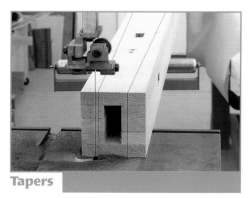

Tapers

Step 6 - Cut the tapers to the dimensions given in the two side view drawings. Use the band saw to make the tapers, staying just outside the lines as shown in Step 6.

Jointing

Step 7 - To remove any saw marks left behind by the band saw, run all four sides of the body through the jointer. Remove small amounts of material with each pass until you reach the proper size of each taper.

Double-Stick Tape

Step 8 - Cut the top hooks (B) to the dimensions given in the material list. Place the pattern of the top hooks on the top of one top hook blank. Use double-stick tape to join the two top hook blanks together.

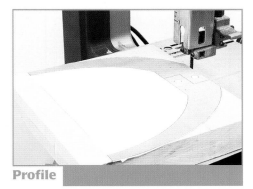

Profile

Step 9 - Use the band saw to gang cut the profile of the top hooks. Only remove material on the outside of the profile lines as shown in Step 9.

Drum Sanding

Step 10 - Keep the two top hook blanks taped together and keep the pattern attached to the blanks. Sand flush to the lines, removing the saw marks left behind by the band saw. Use the drum sander attached in the drill press as shown in Step 10.

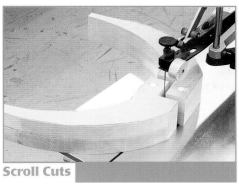

Scroll Cuts

Step 11 - To split the top hooks so that there are four individual hooks, use the scroll saw and follow the lines on the center of the pattern as shown in Step 11. Separate the hooks and sand through 220-grit sandpaper.

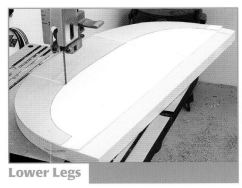

Lower Legs

Step 12 - Cut the upper bottom leg (C) and the lower bottom leg (D) to the dimensions given in the material list. To achieve the given widths, glue-ups may be required. Place the pattern of the lower leg onto the proper blank. Use the band saw to cut out the profile. Repeat method for the upper bottom leg. Drum-sand the two legs as shown in Step 10, and final-sand through 220-grit sandpaper. Split the upper bottom leg as in Step 11 by cutting down through the center following the lines.

Drilling

Step 13 - Sand the body through 220-grit sandpaper. Place the hooks into their mortises. Drill into the hooks through the pre-drilled dowel holes on the body as shown in Step 13. Repeat the steps for the upper and lower legs.

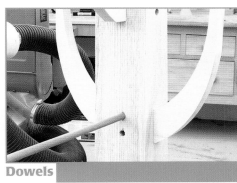

Dowels

Step 14 - Place glue into the holes and slide the respective dowels into their positions as shown here in Step 14. Make any necessary adjustments. Finish the coat rack with several coats of Watco Oil.

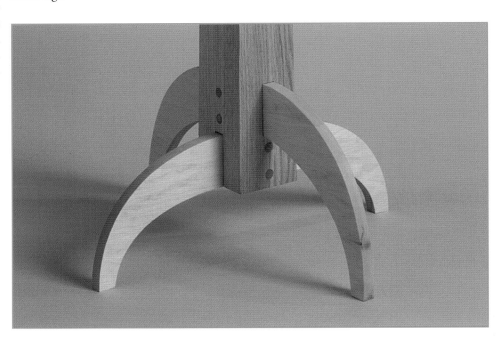

Side View A

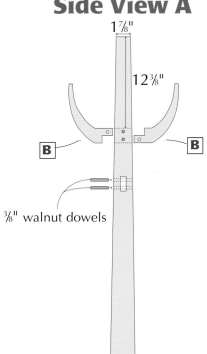

$1\frac{7}{8}$"

$12\frac{3}{8}$"

B

B

$\frac{3}{8}$" walnut dowels

A

$\frac{1}{2}$"

$3\frac{3}{4}$"

D

Detail Top

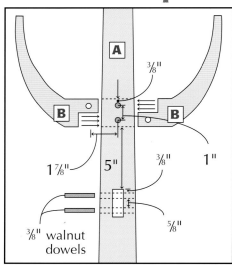

A

$\frac{3}{8}$"

B

B

$1\frac{7}{8}$"

5"

$\frac{3}{8}$"

1"

$\frac{3}{8}$" walnut dowels

$\frac{5}{8}$"

Side View B

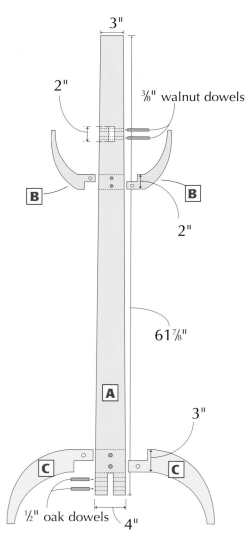

3"

2"

$\frac{3}{8}$" walnut dowels

B

B

2"

$61\frac{7}{8}$"

A

3"

C

C

$\frac{1}{2}$" oak dowels

4"

Detail Bottom

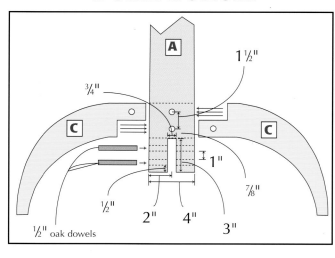

A

$1\frac{1}{2}$"

$\frac{3}{4}$"

C

C

1"

$\frac{7}{8}$"

$\frac{1}{2}$"

2"

4"

3"

$\frac{1}{2}$" oak dowels

Mirror and Shelf

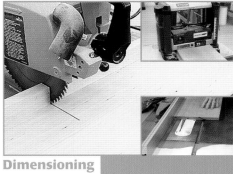

Dimensioning

Step 1 - Cut the stiles (A), top rail (B), bottom rail (C), shelf (D) and shelf supports (E) to the dimensions given in the material list. Use the radial arm saw, table saw, and planer if necessary to make each piece as shown in Step 1 and Step 1 insets.

Stile Miters

Step 2 - The top ends of the stiles receive 45-degree miters, as shown in the front view drawing. Use the table saw with the miter gauge to make each miter as shown in Step 2.

Rail Miters

Step 3 - The ends of the top rail receive 45-degree miters to match the miters in the stiles. Use the table saw and miter gauge to make each miter as shown in Step 3.

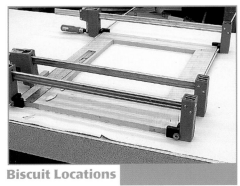

Biscuit Locations

Step 4 - The #10 biscuits (J) are used in the 45-degree miters and in the bottom rail. Refer to the front view drawing for biscuit locations and transfer them to the dry-fitted and clamped frame as shown in Step 4.

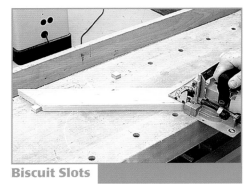

Biscuit Slots

Step 5 - Disassemble the frame and use the biscuit joiner to mill each slot in the stiles and rails as shown in Step 5.

Material List			**T x W x L**
A stiles	(cherry)	2	¾" x 3" x 27"
B top rail	(cherry)	1	¾" x 3" x 20"
C bottom rail	(cherry)	1	¾" x 7" x 14"
D shelf	(cherry)	1	¾" x 4" x 18"
E shelf supports*	(cherry)	2	¾" x 3" x 3"
F top	(cherry)	1	1¼" x 2" x 22½"

Supply List			
G mirror with 1" bevel		1	¼" x 14½" x 17½"
H mirror spacers	(pine)	4	1/16" x 1/16" x 1"
I wooden plugs	(cherry)	2	⅜" diam. x ⅜"
J biscuits		6	#10
K wood screws		8	#6 x 1⅝"
L wood glue			
M silicone II			
N double-sided tape			
O masking tape			
P glazing points			
Q hooks		3	solid brass
R finish			Danish natural oil

*See Pattern Packet.

Laminating

Step 6 - To achieve the top's (F) thickness, two blanks are laminated together using wood glue (L) and clamps as shown in Step 6. Once the glue has cured, mill the blank to its final dimensions given in the material list.

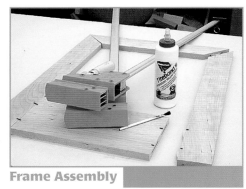

Frame Assembly

Step 7 - Use wood glue, #10 biscuits and some clamps to fasten the rail and stiles together, checking for square as shown in Step 7.

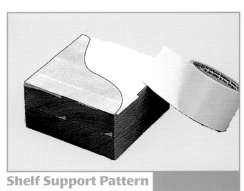

Shelf Support Pattern

Step 8 - Locate the shelf support pattern and adhere it to the two ganged supports (E) with double-sided tape (N) as shown in Step 8.

Front View Drawing

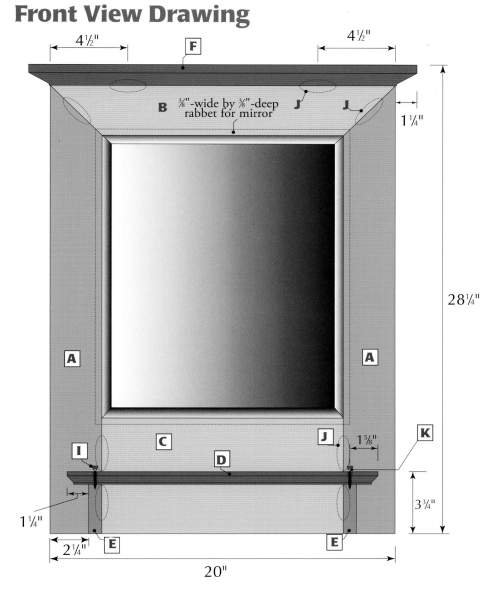

4½" F 4½"

B ⅜"-wide by ⅜"-deep
rabbet for mirror J J

1¼"

28¼"

A A

I C J 1⅝" K

D 3¾"

1¼" E E

2¼" 20"

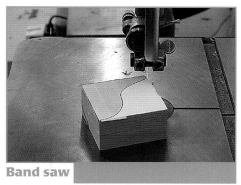

Band saw

Step 9 - Use the band saw to cut out the ganged shelf supports as shown in Step 9.

Drum Sanding

Step 10 - Use the drum sander on the ganged shelf supports to sand smooth the saw marks left behind from the band saw as shown in Step 10.

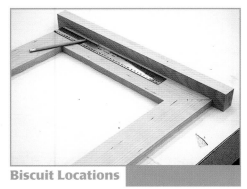

Biscuit Locations

Step 11 - The top attaches to the top rail with two #10 biscuits. Center the top on the rail with the backs flush. Mark two evenly spaced biscuit slot locations, as shown in Step 11.

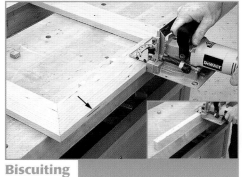

Biscuiting

Step 12 - Use the biscuit joiner to make each slot in the top rail and top blank as shown in Step 12 and Step 12 inset.

Shelf Support Pattern

Step 13 - The top blank receives a chamfer along its sides and front edge. Use the router table and router with a chamfering bit to make the profile as shown in Step 13. The depth of the cut is of your choice.

Chamfering Shelf

Step 14 - The shelf's bottom sides and front edge receive a chamfer that matches the top blank. Use the router table and router with the same chamfering bit as in Step 13 to mill the profile, as shown in Step 14.

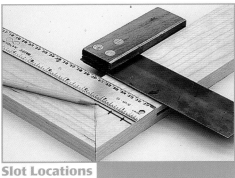

Slot Locations

Step 15 - The project is hung on the wall with two slot holes in the back rail that are 16" apart, centered 1" down from the top rail's top edge. Mark a start and stop location as shown in Step 15.

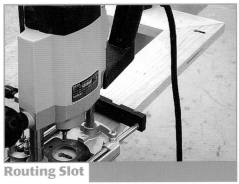

Routing Slot

Step 16 - Use a handheld router with a ⅜" slot hanging bit to make the two slots in the top rail as shown in Step 16.

Support Screw Locations

Step 17 - The shelf supports are attached to the stiles with glue and wood screws (K). Refer to the front view drawing and side view drawing for screw hole locations in the stiles. Use the drill press with a countersinking bit to pre-drill each hole on the stile's back as shown in Step 17.

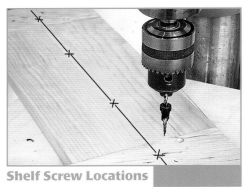

Shelf Screw Locations

Step 18 - The shelf is screwed to the bottom rail and stiles. Evenly space four screws along the back side of the rail and stiles. Refer to the side view drawing for screw height locations. Use the drill press with the same countersinking bit to pre-drill each screw hole as shown in Step 18.

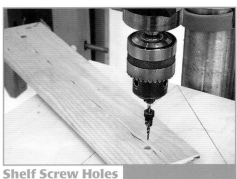

Shelf Screw Holes

Step 19 - The shelf is attached to the shelf supports with two wood screws (K). Refer to the front view drawing and side view drawing for screw hole locations. Use the drill press with a ⅜" countersinking bit to pre-drill and countersink for ⅜" wood plugs (I) as shown in Step 19.

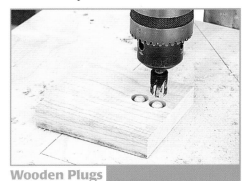

Wooden Plugs

Step 20 - Use the drill press with a ⅜" plug-cutting bit to mill two wooden plugs from a scrap piece of cherry as shown in Step 20. Now is a good time to sand all of the pieces through 220-grit sandpaper.

Mirror Rabbet

Step 21 - The mirror (G) sits in a ⅜"-wide by ⅜"-deep rabbet milled into the back of the frame. Use the router table and router with a ⅜" rabbeting bit to make the rabbet as shown in Step 21. Make a few passes to remove the material to help prevent tear-out. Use a sharp chisel to square up the corners.

Attaching Top

Step 22 - Attach the top to the top rail with the biscuits, glue and clamps as shown in Step 22. Make sure to measure diagonally to check the frame for square.

Attaching Shelf Support

Step 23 - Attach the shelf supports to the stiles with glue and screws as shown in Step 23. To help hold the support in position, a spring clamp was used. Refer to the front view drawing for support location.

Attaching Shelf

Step 24 - Attach the shelf to the shelf supports with some wood glue and screws as shown in Step 24. Attach the shelf assembly, centered on the bottom rail and stiles with screws and glue as shown in Step 24 inset.

Finish

Step 25 - Finish the project with a few coats of Danish natural oil (R) as shown in Step 25. Make sure that no oil gets into the rabbet on the back side of the frame. Use masking tape (O) to mask the rabbet.

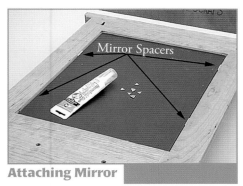

Attaching Mirror

Step 26 - Attach the mirror to the rabbet with silicone (M). Run a bead on the rabbet. Center the mirror in the rabbet, pressing firmly on the mirror to adhere it to the silicone. Run another bead around the edges of the mirror as shown in Step 26.

Attaching Hooks

Step 27 - If the mirror is slightly undersized, use the mirror spacers (H) to help keep the mirror centered. For added support, put in a few glazing points (P).

Attach the three brass hooks (Q), evenly spaced between the shelf supports as shown in Step 27.

Side View Drawing

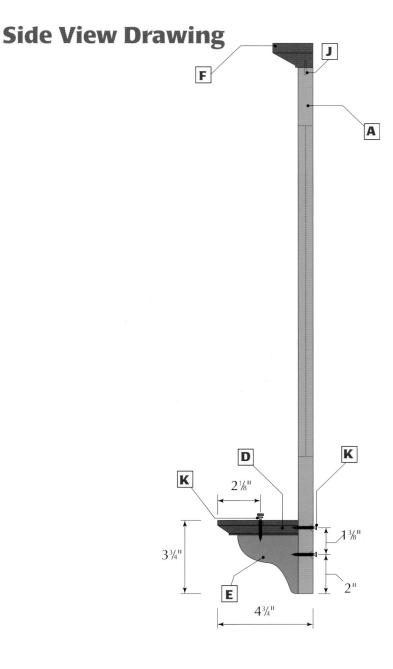

Hall Tree

Step 1 - Cut the stiles (A), bottom rail (B), middle rail (C) and top rail (D) to the dimensions given in the material list. A rabbet is milled along the inside back of each stile. Using the table saw with a sacrificial fence and a ¼" dado blade, mill the ¼"-wide by ¼"-deep rabbets as shown in Step 1.

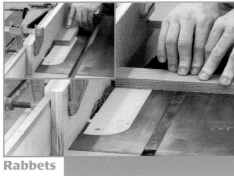

Rabbets

Step 2 - A couple of rabbets are milled into each rail. With the table saw still set up, raise the blade to ½" and mill the two ends on each piece, as shown in Step 2. Lower the blade back down to a ¼" and flip the pieces over. For the middle rail, a rabbet is milled along both inside long edges.

For the bottom rail, a rabbet is milled on the inside top long edge, as shown in Step 2 inset. For the top rail, a rabbet is milled along the bottom long edge.

Panel

Step 3 - Cut the back panel (F) to the dimensions given in the material list as shown in Step 3.

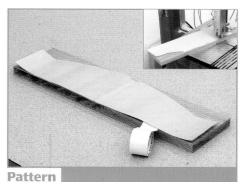

Pattern

Step 4 - Locate the pattern of the top rail and affix to the front side of the top rail as shown in Step 4. Use the band saw to cut the profile out, as shown in Step 4 inset. Use the drum sander to clean up the edges.

Panel Assembly

Step 5 - Lay out the panel pieces and dry clamp them together as shown in Step 5. Place the back panel in position to help keep it square. Make any final adjustments if necessary. Spread glue into the rabbets on the rails and into the rabbets on the stiles where the two come together. Check for square and set aside to dry. Refer to the drawing on page 36 for further reference.

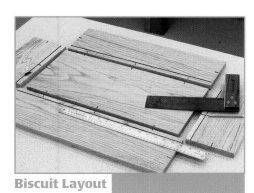

Biscuit Layout

Step 6 - Cut the box front (H), sides (I), back (J) and bottom (K) to the dimensions given in the material list. When the box is constructed, the bottom is recessed ¼" from the sides, front and back. Refer to the drawing on page 33 for all biscuit locations. Use a square, ruler and pencil to make the layout marks as shown in Step 6.

Material List			T x W x L
A stiles	(oak)	2	¾" x 3" x 70"
B bottom rail	(oak)	1	¾" x 3¾" x 18½"
C middle rail	(oak)	1	¾" x 2½" x 18½"
D top rail*	(oak)	1	¾" x 4¾" x 18½"
E base	(oak)	1	¾" x 11¼" x 25½"
F back panel	(oak bead board)	1	¼" x 18½" x 41½"
G legs*	(oak)	2	3" x 3" x 31½"
Box List			
H front	(oak)	1	¾" x 5½" x 22"
I sides	(oak)	2	¾" x 5½" x 9½"
J back	(oak)	1	¾" x 5½" x 20½"
K bottom	(oak)	1	¾" x 8¾" x 20½"
L top	(oak)	1	¾" x 1¼" x 22¼"
M lid	(oak)	1	¾" x 9½" x 22¼"
Supply List			
N hat/coat brass hangers**		2	#127414
O brass cabinet hinges**		2	#16R38
P mirror		1	¼" x 18½" x 20½"
Q mirror clips		4	
R biscuits		3	#10
S biscuits		12	#20
T brads			⅝"
U wood screws		12	#6 x 1⅝"
V brass wood screws		4	#6 x ⅝"

* This item is available from Home Depot and is called "Newell Starter Posts"
** These items are available from Woodcraft® Stores. For more information, call 800-225-1153, or visit their web site at **www.woodcraft.com**.

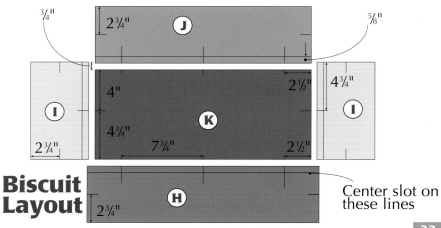

Biscuit Layout

Center slot on these lines

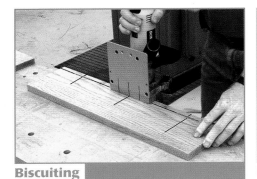

Biscuiting

Step 7 - Use the biscuit joiner to make all of the biscuits in the box blanks. For the bottom to be recessed ¼", the biscuits must be raised a further ¼" from the bottom edges of the front, back and sides as shown in Step 8.

Box Assembly

Step 8 - The box is fastened together using glue and clamps, as shown in Step 8. Be sure to spread the glue along the end and side edges of each piece and also in the biscuits' slots.

Base

Step 9 - Cut the base (E) to the dimensions given in the material list. On the bottom of each leg, there is a ¾"-wide by ¾"-long tenon. The tenon will sit in the mortises milled in the base. Refer to the drawing on page 36. Use a ruler and compass to mark the locations as shown in Step 9. Use the drill press with a ¾" Forstner bit to make the through mortises.

Countersinking

Step 10 - The base receives five evenly spaced countersunk holes along the bottom side of the back edge. Use the drill press to mill the holes as shown in Step 10. Refer to front view drawing on page 36 for hole locations.

Routing Base

Step 11 - A decorative edge is milled around the sides and front top edges of the base. Use the router table with an ogee bit to make the cut as shown in Step 11.

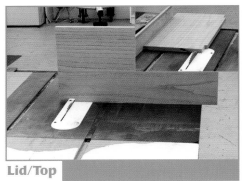

Lid/Top

Step 12 - The lid (M) and top (L) come from one single blank. Cut a ¾" oak blank to 10⅞"- wide by 22¼"- long. The two back ends are notched out to fit around the stiles on the panel. Measure down ½" from the back edge and in 2⅛" from the side edge. Use the table saw to make the notches as shown in Step 12. Use the table saw with a ⅛" blade to cut the lid and top to the dimensions given in the material list as shown in Step 12 inset.

Hinge Locations

Step 13 - The two hinges get mortised into the lid and top. Measure 4" in from the side edges and mark the mortise location as shown in Step 13. Use a router with a straight cutting bit to remove most of the material in the mortise and a chisel to square up the corners.

Routing Lid/Top

Step 14 - The same decorative bit that was used on the base is also used on the lid and top. Use the router table to mill the top front and side edges as shown in Step 14.

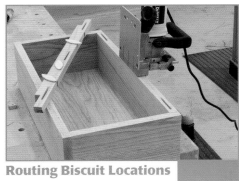

Routing Biscuit Locations

Step 15 - The top is fastened to the box with three #10 biscuits (R). Center the top onto the back edge of the box and mark three biscuit locations. Use the biscuit joiner to make the slots as shown in Step 15.

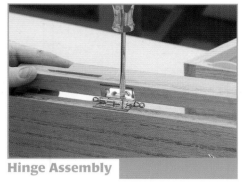

Hinge Assembly

Step 16 - Now is a good time to sand all pieces through 220-grit sandpaper.

Pre-drill for the brass screws that come with the hinges. Screw both hinges in place as shown in Step 16. Be careful not to break the soft brass screws.

Gluing

Step 17 - Use glue in the slots for the biscuits and also along the back edge. Clamp the top to the box and set aside to dry as shown in Step 17.

Panel Assembly

Step 18 - Use brads (T) to fasten the back panel to the stiles. Shoot the brads at a slight angle to ensure that they won't show from the front as shown in Step 18.

Base Assembly

Step 19 - With the panel flat on the work table, center the base on the bottom edge of the panel. Pre-drill through the countersunk holes in the base into the panel. Use wood screws (U) to attach the base to the panel as shown in Step 19.

Box/Panel Assembly

Step 20 - Cut the legs (G) to the dimensions given in the material list. Place the leg tenons in the mortises in the base. Set the bottom of the box on top of the legs. Center and clamp the box to the panel and check for square. Make any adjustments as necessary. Pre-drill through the back side of the panel stiles into the sides of the box for wood screws. Fasten the box to panel using wood screws as shown in Step 20.

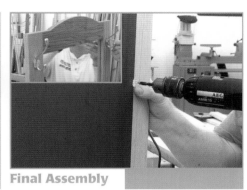

Final Assembly

Step 21 - From inside the box, locate the center where the legs meet the bottom. Countersink into the bottom, making sure to hold the legs tight up against the front and sides of the box. Use wood screws to fasten the legs to the bottom.

Finish the piece with several coats of oil. Place the mirror (P) into position and fasten it in place with glass clips (Q) as shown in Step 21. Pre-drill and fasten the hat and coat hangers (N) as shown in Step 21 inset.

Front View

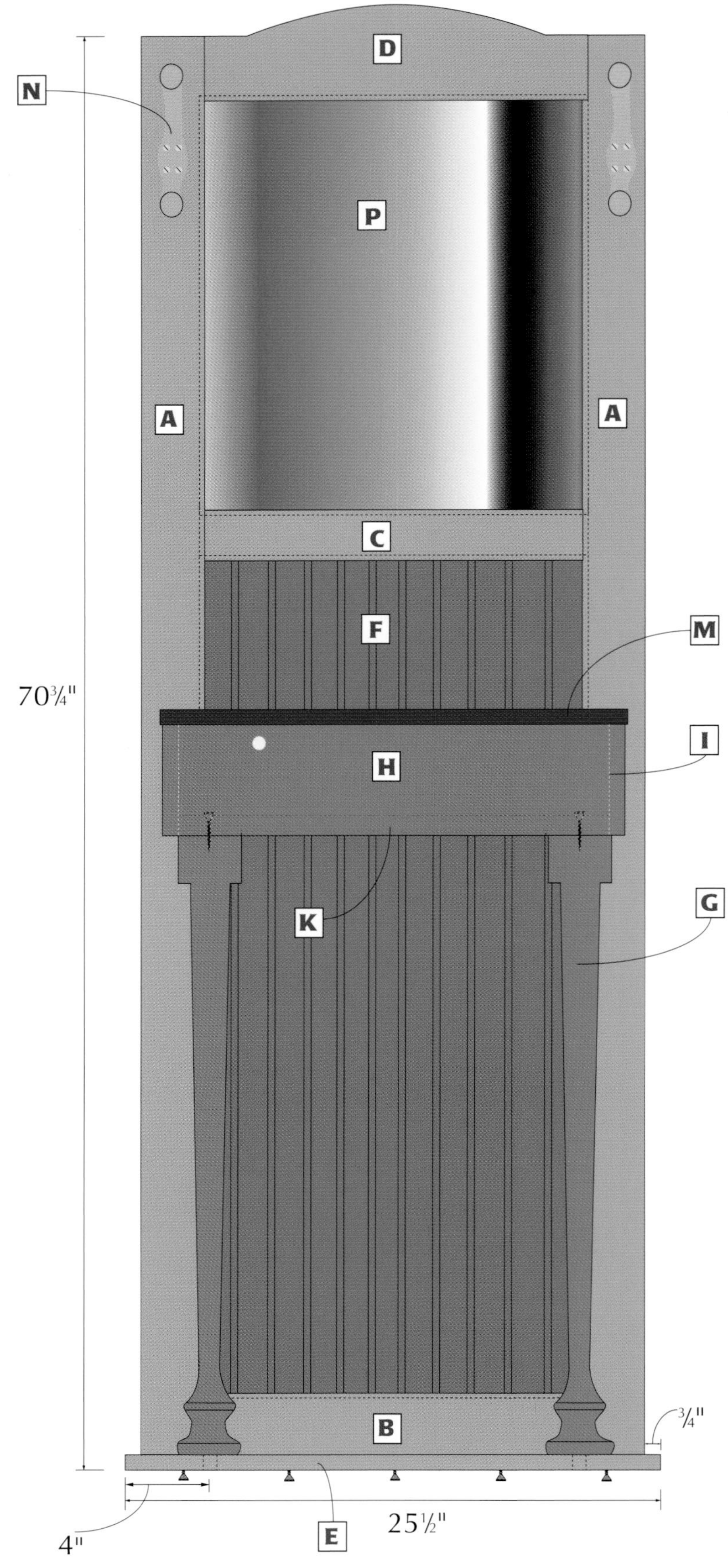

Side View

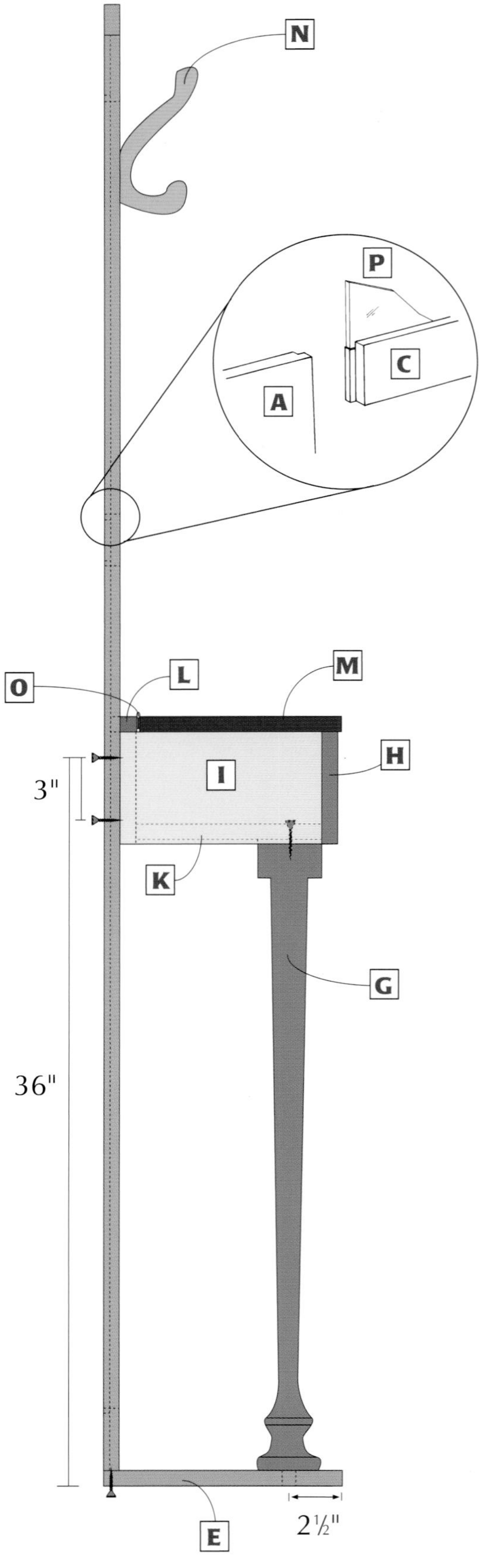

N

D

N

P

A   A

P

C

A

C

C

F

M

70¾"   M   L   O

I   H

I   G

H

3"   I

K   K

G

B   G

¾"

E   36"

4"   25½"   E   2½"

E

Kitchen Island

We call this project a kitchen island, but after its completion, we decided that it could be used in a craft room, sewing room or any place that requires the ease of a cart that moves around. So don't let the title fool you; we're sure you have some room in your house for this handy cart on wheels.

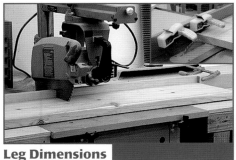

Leg Dimensions

Step 1 - Cut the legs (A) slightly longer than the dimensions given in the material list. For the thickness we need, the legs are cut from a piece of 1½"-thick stock and ripped to 3" wide as shown in Step 1 and Step 1 inset.

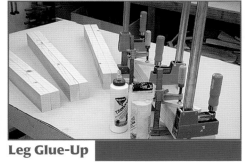

Leg Glue-Up

Step 2 - Use some wood glue (R) and lots of clamps to gang a pair of legs together as shown in Step 2.

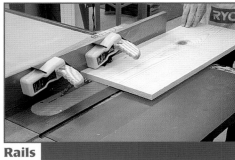

Rails

Step 3 - Cut all of the rails (B-G) to the dimensions given in the material list. Use the radial arm saw to make the crosscuts and the table saw to make the ripped cuts as shown in Step 3.

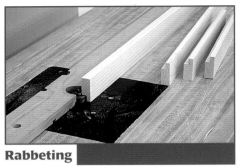

Rabbeting

Step 4 - The middle and bottom rails, both long and short, receive a ⅜"-wide by ½"-deep rabbet along their inside top edge. Use the router in the router table with a rabbeting bit adjusted to make the appropriate rabbet and a fence to add stability as shown in Step 4.

Scraper

Step 5 - After the glue has dried in the legs, use a scraper to remove the squeezed-out glue on each leg as shown in Step 5.

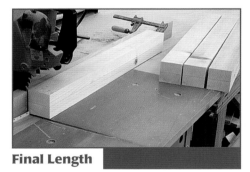

Final Length

Step 6 - Use the radial arm saw to trim both ends of the legs to achieve your final length of 31" as shown in Step 6.

Material List			**T x W x L**
A legs	(pine)	8	3" x 3" x 31"
B bottom long rails	(pine)	2	¾" x 2" x 28¼"
C bottom short rails	(pine)	2	¾" x 2" x 13½"
D middle long rails	(pine)	2	¾" x 1½" x 28¼"
E middle short rails	(pine)	2	¾" x 1½" x 13½"
F top long rails	(pine)	2	¾" x 2" x 28¼"
G top short rails	(pine)	2	¾" x 2" x 13½"
H bottom shelf	(birch plywood)	1	½" x 15" x 29¾"
I middle shelf	(birch plywood)	1	½" x 15" x 29¾"
J top	(maple)	11	1¾" x 1¾" x 36"
K center drawer divider	(maple)	1	¾" x 8" x 15¾"
L side drawer guides	(maple)	2	½" x ½" x 12"
M upper drawer guides	(pine)	2	¾" x 3" x 14¼"
N top mounting clips	(pine)	6	¾" x 2" x 2"
O drawer fronts	(maple)	4	¾" x 5¹⁵⁄₁₆" x 12¹⁵⁄₁₆"
P drawer sides	(maple)	4	½" x 5¹⁵⁄₁₆" x 15"
Q drawer bottoms	(birch plywood)	2	¼" x 12⁷⁄₁₆" x 15"

Supply List			
R wood glue			waterproof
S biscuits		4	#10
T center drawer divider wood screws		5	#6 x 1¼"
U maple buttons		2	½"
V brads			¾"
W wood filler			
X American Accents paint (pint)			hunt club green (satin finish)
Y butcher block oil			
Z Watco Oil			natural
AA drawer pulls		4	
BB mounting clip wood screws		6	#6 x 1⅝"
CC Varathane spray finish			
DD wheels			1¾" x 2¼" x 2¾"

Witness Marks

Step 7 - It's always best to make the mortises in the legs first; then the tenons on the rails are made to fit. Start by marking each leg right front, left front, right back and left back. Arrange the legs so the best sides are facing out. The inside faces are where the mortises will be made. Mark each face to avoid confusing yourself as shown in Step 7.

Ganging Legs

Step 8 - Start by making mortises for the long rails. Lay the legs flat with the correct side facing up. Align their bottom edges so that they are all flush and clamped together as shown in Step 8.

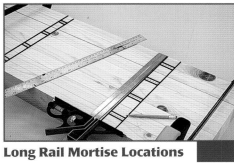

Long Rail Mortise Locations

Step 9 - Mark each leg with a top and bottom. Refer to the front and side view drawings for the long rail locations. Using a square and ruler, mark each mortise location on the legs as shown in Step 9.

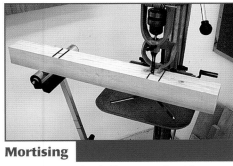

Mortising

Step 10 - Use the drill press with a ⅜" mortising chisel to make the mortises in each leg down to a depth of ¾" as shown in step 10. If you don't have a mortising attachment for your drill press, a series of ⅜" holes drilled to a depth of ¾" will work as well. A sharp chisel will be used to square up the edges.

Short Rail Mortise Locations

Step 11 - Lay the legs flat with the short rail mortise side facing up and their bottom edges flush with one another. Clamp all four legs together. Refer to the front and side view drawings for mortise locations. Transfer the locations to the legs as shown in step 11.

Side View

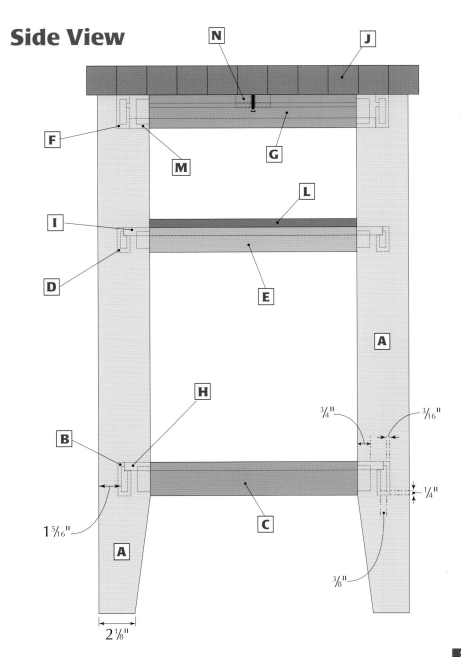

Front View

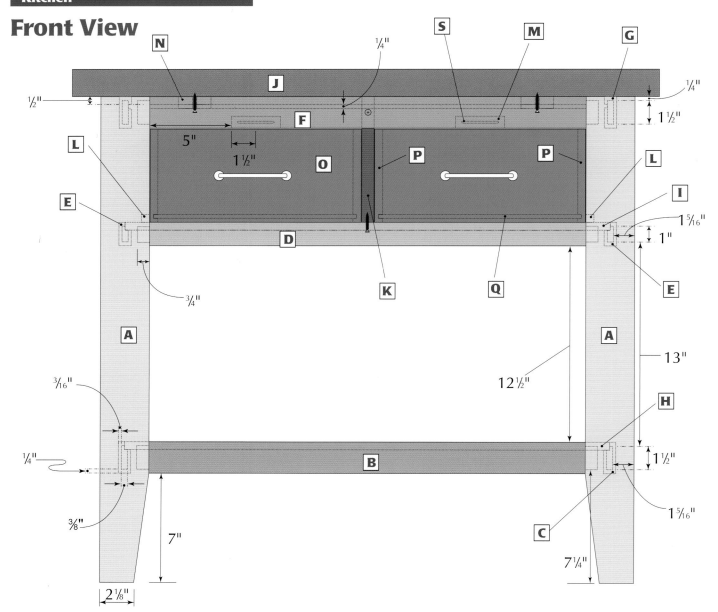

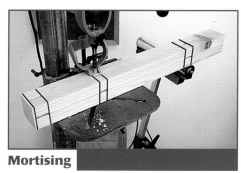

Mortising

Step 12 - Use the same mortising chisel and dimensions that were used in step 10 to make the short rail mortises as shown in Step 12.

Taper Locations

Step 13 - The bottom of the legs each receive a taper on their inside faces. Stand the legs up in the final order. Notice how the tapers are going to be on the same face as the mortises. Refer to the front and side view drawings for taper locations. Transfer locations to each leg as shown in Step 13.

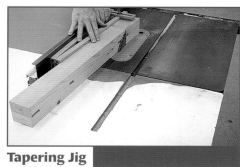

Tapering Jig

Step 14 - Use the table saw with a tapering jig to make each taper as shown in Step 14. If your table saw blade does not rise high enough, use the band saw and then the jointer (to smooth the cut) to make the tapers.

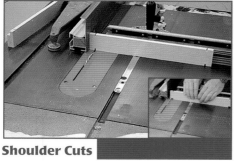

Shoulder Cuts

Step 15 - Use the table saw with the fence and miter gauge to cut the tenons in each of the rails. Refer to the front and side view drawings for tenon dimensions. Make a test tenon in some scrap wood to assure proper fitting. Start off by making the shoulder cuts. Pass each piece through the blade several times, moving the piece further from the fence with each pass to remove the remaining material as shown in Step 15 inset.

Cheek Cuts

Step 16 - Lay the rails flat against the table saw surface and make the cheek cuts, nibbling away the material with each pass as shown in Step 16.

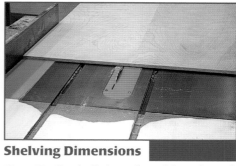

Shelving Dimensions

Step 17 - Sand all the rails and legs through 220-grit sandpaper.

Step 18 - Cut the middle shelf (I) and the bottom shelf (H) to the dimensions given in the material list. Use the table saw to make the cuts as shown in Step 18.

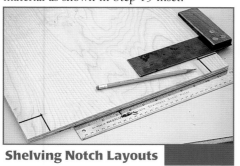

Shelving Notch Layouts

Step 19 - The shelves have notches cut out of their corners to fit around the legs. Dry-fit the rails and legs together and measure around the inside corner of each leg to get the notches' dimensions. Transfer the dimensions to the shelves as shown in Step 19.

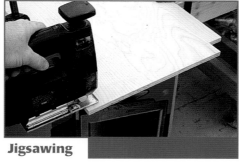

Jigsawing

Step 20 - Use a handheld jigsaw to remove the notches in the shelves as shown in Step 20.

Groove For Mounting Clips

Step 21 - The top rails, both long and short, receive a groove near their top inside edges. The groove is used with top mounting clips (N) to fasten the top to the frame. Use the table saw with a stacked dado blade to make the 1/4"-wide by 1/4"-deep groove down from the top edge as shown in Step 21.

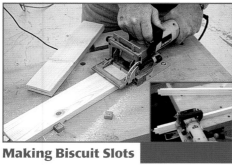

Making Biscuit Slots

Step 22 - Cut the upper drawer guides (M) to the dimensions given in the material list. These guides connect to the front and back top long rails with #10 biscuits (S). Refer to the front view drawing and exploded view drawing for their locations. Mark the biscuit slot locations in each piece, and use the biscuit joiner to make the #10 slots as shown in Step 22 and Step 22 inset.

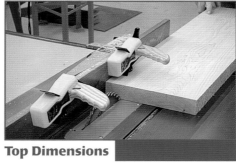

Top Dimensions

Step 23 - Cut the top (J) to the dimensions given in the material list. Cut the top's length about 1" longer than what's given in the material list. Use the radial arm saw to crosscut the pieces and the table saw to make the ripped cuts as shown in Step 23.

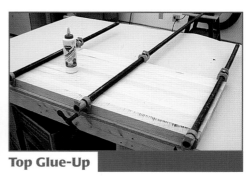

Top Glue-Up

Step 24 - Glue and clamp the top pieces with their side grain face up as shown in Step 24.

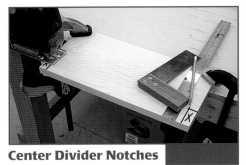

Center Divider Notches

Step 25 - Cut the drawer divider (K) to the dimensions given in the material list. The divider is notched to fit around the top front and back long rails. The notches measure ¾"-wide by 2"- long. Transfer each notch to the divider's top edge as shown in Step 25. Remove the material using the handheld jigsaw.

Step 26 - Cut the side drawer guides (L) to the dimensions given in the material list.

Mounting Clips

Step 27 - Cut the top mounting clips (N) to the dimensions given in the material list. The clips are made with a ¼"-wide by ¼"-long tenon. Use the router in the router table with the fence to make the rabbet in a piece of stock long enough to make the 6 clips as shown in Step 27. The clips are pre-drilled and countersunk in their centers for the wood screws (BB) as shown in Step 27 inset.

Drawer Front Rabbets

Step 28 - Cut the drawer fronts (O), the drawer sides (P) and the drawer bottoms (Q) to the dimensions given in the material list. The drawer fronts receive a ½"-wide by ⅜"-deep rabbet on both their inside ends. Use the table saw with a ½" stacked dado blade raised to a height of ⅜". Use a miter gauge to keep the fronts square as you run them over the blade as shown in Step 28.

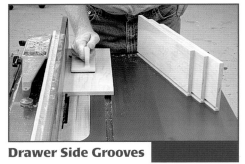

Drawer Side Grooves

Step 29 - The drawer sides' inside surfaces receive a groove along their bottom edges to house the bottom. Make the ¼"-wide by ¼"-deep groove with the table saw and a ¼" stacked dado blade. The grooves start ¼" up from their bottom edges as shown in Step 29.

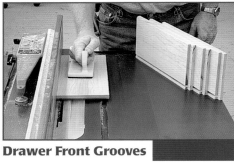

Drawer Front Grooves

Step 30 - The drawer front's inside surface receives the same groove along its bottom edge, except it's ⅜" deep as shown in Step 30. Sand all of the drawer parts through 220-grit sandpaper.

Top Edge Round Over

Step 31 - Sand the top through 220-grit sandpaper. Cut the top down to its final length of 36." Use a round-over bit in the router to ease the edges of the top. Both top and bottom edges get rounded over as shown in Step 31.

Top Rail Button Locations

Step 32 - The center drawer divider is held in place with two wood screws (T) through the top long front and back rails and three wood screws (T) centered and evenly spaced through the middle shelf. Locate the center on the long rails, and drill a ½" countersunk hole 1" down from the top edge. Countersink to a depth to hold a ½" maple button (U) as shown in Step 32.

Middle Shelf Screw Locations

Step 33 - Drill three evenly spaced countersunk screw holes in the center of the middle shelf's bottom side. Only countersink to a depth to allow the screw head to sit flush with the wood as shown in Step 33.

Partial Glue-Up

Step 34 - Assemble the project frame in two halves. Clamp and glue two legs with the top long rail, middle long rail and bottom long rail. The groove in the top rail and the rabbets in the middle and bottom rails face toward the top as shown in Step 34. Check for square.

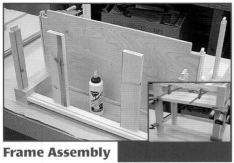

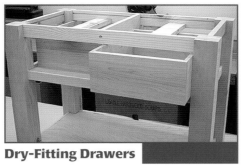

Frame Assembly

Step 35 - Once the two halves have dried, keep one set of legs flat against the table. Glue in place the short rails and upper drawer guides with biscuits in one half of the leg assembly. Place the middle shelf in position now as shown in Step 35. Glue the other leg assembly onto the short rails and upper drawer guides with biscuits. Clamp the entire frame assembly together and check for square as shown in Step 35 inset.

Dry-Fitting Drawers

Step 36 - Dry-fit the drawers together. Place the center divider into its final position. Slide the drawers in the openings. Check that the clearance is enough side to side and up and down as shown in Step 36. Make any necessary adjustments if the drawers don't move freely.

Fastening Middle Shelf

Step 37 - Remove the drawers and fasten the middle shelf to the top rails with ¾" brads (V) as shown in Step 37. Cover the nail heads with wood filler (W). Sand the wood filler flush when dry.

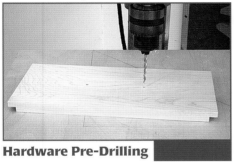

Hardware Pre-Drilling

Step 38 - Pre-drill in the center of the drawer fronts for the screws that will hold your hardware in place as shown in Step 38.

Drawer Assembly

Step 39 - Assemble the drawers together with some wood glue in the rabbets and ¾" brads (V) as shown in Step 39.

Mounting Clips Screw Locations

Step 40 - Place the top, with the top side down, and center the frame assembly on the top. Place the top mounting clips into position, evenly spread around the top. Mark the clip screw locations with an awl through the screw holes in the clips as shown in Step 40.

Pre-Drilling

Step 41 - Remove the frame assembly and pre-drill into the top for the 1⅝" mounting clip wood screws (BB) as shown in Step 41.

Tape Off and Paint

Step 42 - The entire project is painted except the top, drawers, drawer divider, upper drawer guides, side drawer guides and maple buttons. Paint the project a color of your choice or use the color we used (X), as shown in Step 42. The middle shelf's top surface is not painted between the two side drawer guides and the front and back long rails. Use some tape to prevent painting on these areas.

Applying Finish

Step 43 - Finish the painted portion of the project with a few coats of the spray finish (CC) as shown in Step 43.

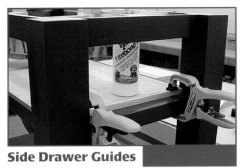

Side Drawer Guides

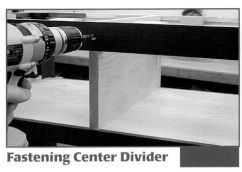

Fastening Center Divider

Attaching Top and Wheels

Step 44 - Remove the tape from the middle shelf. Glue and clamp in place the side drawer guides so that their inside edges are flush with the inside edges of the legs as shown in Step 44.

Step 45 - Center and attach the center drawer divider with wood screws (T) from under the middle shelf and through the long front and back rails as shown in Step 45.

Step 46 - Place the frame assembly back onto the top, and fasten the top to the frame through the mounting clips with the wood screws (BB). Attach the wheels (DD) with four screws centered on the bottom of each leg as shown in Step 46 inset.

Step 47 - Apply a coat of butcher block oil (Y) to the top. Add a few coats of Watco Oil (Z) to the center divider, drawer fronts, drawer sides (on their outside surfaces only) and the maple buttons. Attach hardware (AA) to the drawer fronts.

Exploded View

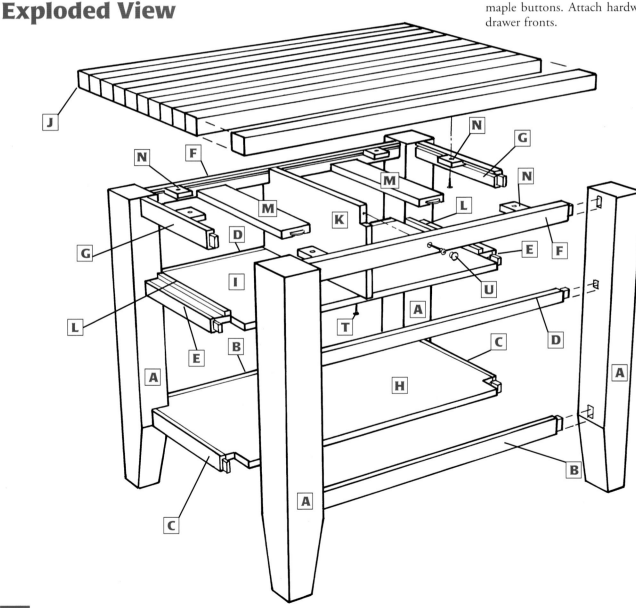

Cork Board With Shelf

Backing

Step 1 - Cut the cork backing (D) and cork (E) to the dimensions given in the material list. Use the table saw to make the cuts as shown in Step 1.

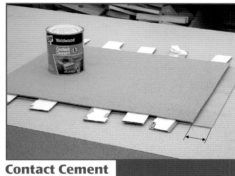

Contact Cement

Step 2 - Align the top edges of the cork and cork backing. There should be about a 1⅜" overhang of the cork backing along the bottom edge. Adhere the cork to the cork backing with some contact cement (K). Use some strips of cardboard to assist in aligning the cork to the cork backing as shown in Step 2.

Hanging Slot Bit

Step 3 - The mantle/shelf (C) receives a couple of hanging slot grooves on both back side corners. Refer to the front view drawing for slot locations. Use the router with a slot bit to make the slots as shown in Step 3.

Mantle Rabbet

Step 4 - The top back side edge on the mantle/shelf receives a stopped rabbet. The rabbet is the same size as the overhang on the cork backing. Center the cork backing on the mantle/shelf and mark its stopped locations. Use a router and a straight cutting bit set to a depth of ⅛" to remove the material as shown in Step 4.

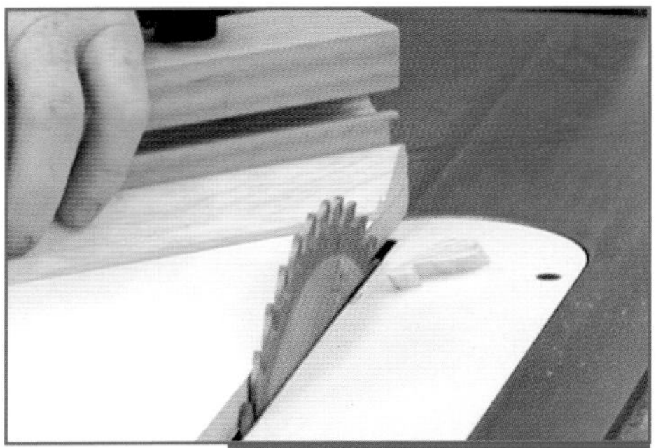

Side Miters

Step 5 - Cut the sides (A) and top (B) to the dimensions given in the material list. The top ends of the sides are mitered to 45 degrees; use the table saw and miter sliding table to make the cuts as shown in Step 5.

Material List				T x W x L
A	sides	(top base molding)	2	¹¹/₁₆" x 1⅜" x 24⅞"
B	top	(top base molding)	1	¹¹/₁₆" x 1⅜" x 20¼"
C	mantle/shelf	(pine)	1	3¼" x 3¼" x 23½"
D	cork backing	(plywood)	1	⅛" x 18" x 25⅛"
Supply List				
E	cork			¼" x 18" x 23¾"
F	brads			18 ga. x ½"
G	brads			18 ga. x 1"
H	wood glue			
I	spray paint for undercoat (Design Master, October Brown)			
J	spray paint for topcoat (Design Master, Ivory)			
K	contact cement			
L	masking tape			

Top Miters

Step 6 - The ends of the top (B) are also mitered to 45 degrees as shown in Step 6. Refer to the front view drawing for miter reference.

Rabbets

Step 7 - Mill ¼"-wide by ⅜"-deep through rabbets along the inside back edge of the sides and top as shown in Step 7.

Fastening

Step 8 - Place glue in the miters of the top and sides. Place the cork and cork backing into the rabbets of the sides and top. Nail the ½" brads (F) through the backing and into the sides and top as shown in Step 8.

Final Assembly

Step 9 - Attach the cork backing to the back side of the mantle/shelf with the 1" brads (G) and glue. Use a pneumatic nailer and nail several brads across the cork backing and into the mantle/shelf as shown in Step 9.

Taping Off

Step 10 - Mask off the cork with some tape (L) and paper. Spray the undercoat (I) first; let it dry. Spray the top coat (J) and let it dry as shown in Step 10.

Final Sanding

Step 11 - To achieve the worn look, use some sandpaper and sand lightly around the entire project. Continue to sand until the undercoat starts to show as shown in Step 11.

Front View

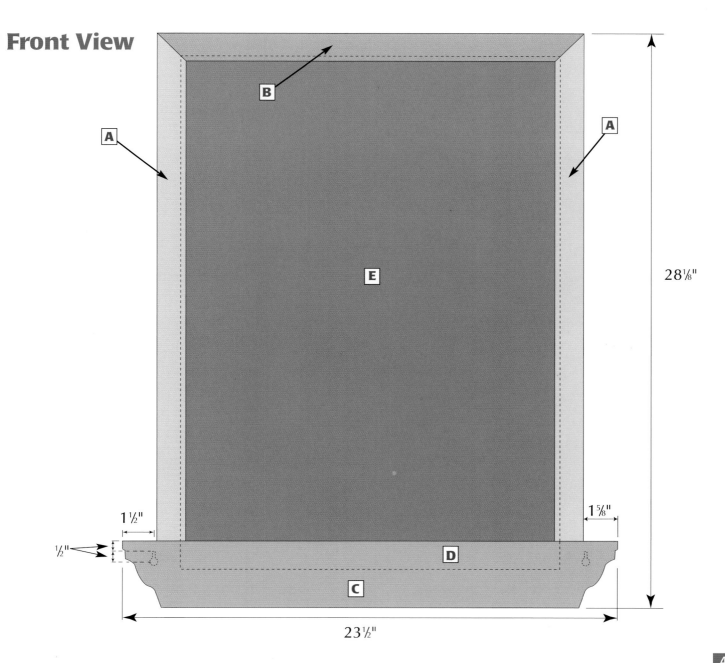

A

B

A

E

28⅛"

1½"

1⅝"

½"

D

C

23½"

Recycle Center

Tired of looking at that mess of disorganized recyclables? Now's your chance to give that space a nice, organized look. This cabinet can do the job for your cans and papers. However, it can also be used to house whatever your imagination can ponder.

Ripping

Step 1 - Rip the bottom (H) and sides (I) to the dimensions given in the material list. Use the table saw to do the ripping as shown in Step 1. When handling such a large piece of plywood, it's best to have two people. However, one person with several dead-men can get the job accomplished. Use the sliding table on the table saw to make the cross-cuts.

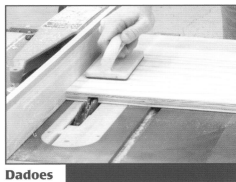

Dadoes

Step 2 - The bottom blank fits into dadoes that are milled on the inside face of the side blanks. Use the stacked dado blade installed to a thickness of ¾" on the table saw. Refer to the front view drawing on page 51 for the locations of the two dadoes. Use the table saw with the proper setting of the fence to mill the dadoes as shown in Step 2.

Partial Assembly

Step 3 - Evenly space out three pre-drilled countersunk holes on the outside of the side blanks. Drill the holes into the center of the dadoes that were milled in Step 2. Apply glue to the dadoes and to the bottom blank edges that rest in the dadoes. Align the bottom and sides so that they are flush in the back (front edge of the bottom will protrude slightly in front). Use the #6 x 1¾" wood screws to fasten the sides to the bottom blank as shown.

Partial Assembly

Step 4 - A face frame is used to cover the end grain of the plywood sides. Cut the face frame rail (E), face frame stiles (F) and face frame center stile (K) to the dimensions given in the material list. Where the stiles and rails meet, #3 biscuits (P) are used to strengthen the joints. Refer to the face frame drawing on page 51 for the orientation of the face frame assembly. Use the biscuit joiner to make the biscuits slots as shown in Step 4. Dowels can also be used in place of biscuits. No glue is applied at this point.

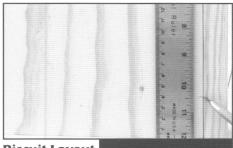

Biscuit Layout

Step 5 - Witness mark the two outside stiles one "left," one "right." Place the stiles on the front edge of the side blanks. Align both the stiles and the sides so that they are both flush at the top. Measure in from the ends 3" and evenly space out five biscuit locations as shown in Step 5. Refer to the face frame drawing on page 51 for layout orientation.

Biscuit Joiner

Step 6 - On the front edge of the bottom blank, evenly space five biscuit locations. Refer to the front view drawing on page 51. To hold the face frame to the sides, #10 biscuit slots are milled in the inside face of the stiles and the front edge of the sides. Use the biscuit joiner to make the biscuit slots.

Material List				T x W x L
A	doors flush overlay	(pine)	2	¾" x 16" x 24⅞"
B	lids	(pine)	2	¾" x 17⅜" x 17½"
C	front base board*	(pine)	1	¾" x 2¼" x 35⅝"
D	side base board	(pine)	2	¾" x 2¼" x 15⅞"
E	face frame rail	(pine)	1	¾" x 1½" x 31⅛"
F	face frame stiles	(pine)	2	¾" x 1½" x 25¾"
G	inside divider	(pine)	2	¾" x 1½" x 14⁵⁄₁₆"
H	bottom	(plywood)	1	¾" x 15⁷⁄₁₆" x 33⅜"
I	sides	(plywood)	2	¾" x 15¹⁄₁₆" x 28"
J	backing	(plywood)	1	⅜" x 27¾" x 34¹⁄₁₆"
K	face frame center stile	(pine)	1	¾" x 1½" x 24¼"
L	inside back rail	(pine)	1	¾" x 1½" x 32⅝"

Supply List			
M	hinges	4	2" for lids
N	wood screws	12	#6 x 1¾"
O	wood buttons	6	½"
P	biscuits		#10, #3
Q	knobs	2	
R	folding support hinge	2	
S	self closing door hinge	4	2"
T	brads	24	1"

*See Pattern Packet.

Dry-Fitting

Step 7 - The top rail and the two outside stiles are fastened together. Spread glue evenly to the biscuit slots on the top rail and the outside stiles, and insert biscuits. Clamp the rail and stiles together, check to make sure they are square and set aside to dry. Once dry, place the biscuits into the biscuit slots on the sides as shown in Step 7. Dry-fit the face frame to the sides and make any necessary adjustments.

Glue-Up

Step 8 - Glue and clamp the two stiles to the side blanks as shown in Step 8. The center stile is placed in position, but is not yet glued in place.

Exploded View

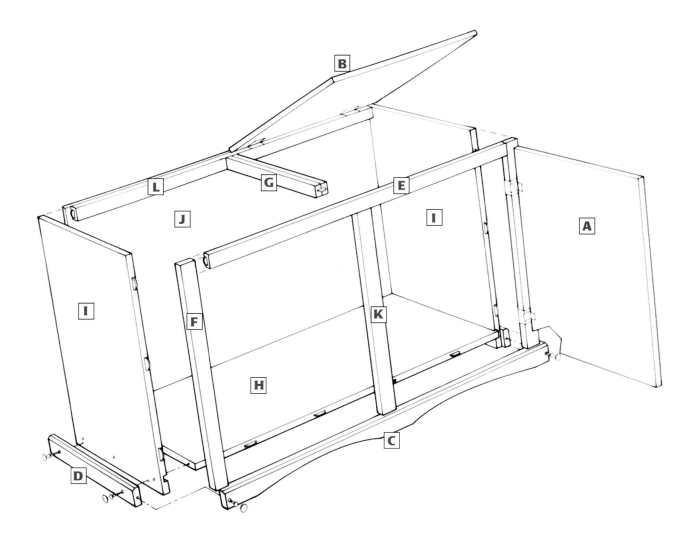

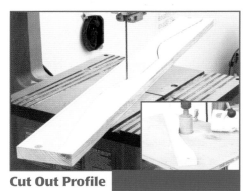

Cut Out Profile

Step 9 - Cut the front base board (C) to the dimensions given in the material list. Use the pattern from the pattern packet to make the profile of the front base board. Use the band saw to make the cuts. Clean up the cuts with the drum sander.

Countersink

Step 10 - Measure in ⅜" and up ¾" on the ends of the front base board to find the locations for the countersunk drill holes.

Chamfering

Step 11 - The outside top facing edge of the front base board has a slight chamfering milled across its length. Use the router table with a chamfering bit to make the cut as shown in Step 11.

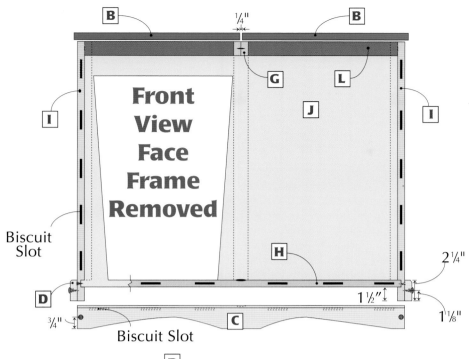

**Front
View
Face
Frame
Removed**

B

B

¼"

G

L

J

I

I

Biscuit
Slot

H

2¼"

D

1½"

¾"

C

1⅛"

Biscuit Slot

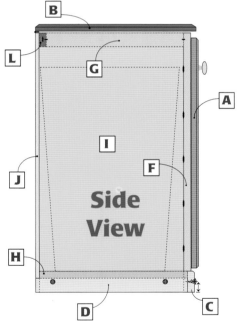

**Side
View**

B

L

G

A

I

F

J

H

D

C

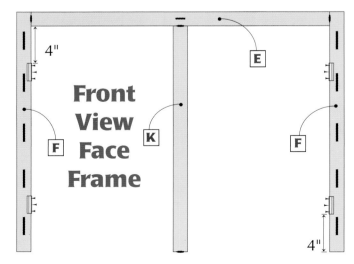

**Front
View
Face
Frame**

4"

E

K

F

F

4"

Side Base Board

Step 12 - Cut the side base boards (D) to the dimensions given in the material list. As in Step 11, the side base boards also receive a chamfering across their outside top-facing edges. Make the cuts using the router table as shown above. Two countersunk holes are evenly spaced on the front side of the side base boards. Use the same bit as in Step 10 to drill the holes. Refer to side view drawing on this page.

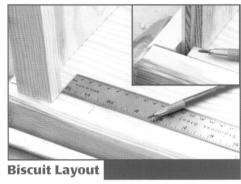

Biscuit Layout

Step 13 - Place and center the front base board into its location. Transfer the biscuit marks from the bottom to the front base board as shown above. Use the biscuit joiner on the inside face of the front base board to make the matching slots.

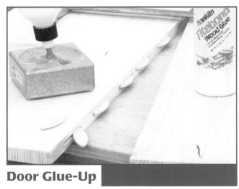

Door Glue-Up

Step 14 - Make the doors (A) and lids (B) by biscuiting and gluing panels together as shown in Step 14. Cut the doors and lids to the dimensions given in the material list once they are dry.

Chamfering

Step 15 - Both the lids and doors receive the same chamfering that was used on the base boards. Chamfer the front side top edges of the four panels, removing very little material. Use the router table as shown above, to make the cuts.

Back Rail

Step 16 - Cut the inside back rail (L) to the dimensions given in the material list. Use biscuits to attach the rail to the top back corner of the sides. Two 2" hinges (M) are used on each lid. Measure in 3" from each side of the lids. Start your hinge mortise at this location to the underside of the lids. Center the lids on top of the assembly. Transfer the location of the hinges to the top edge of the back rail.

Self-Closing Hinges

Step 17 - Self-closing hinges (S) are used to hang the doors. Refer to the front view face frame drawing for location of the hinges.

Center Stile

Step 18 - Dry fit the front base board in place. Mark the location where the center stile meets the front base board and bottom blank. To hold the center stile in place, mill a #3 biscuit slot into the front base board and bottom blank as shown in Step 18. Be sure the center stile is square and straight before cutting the biscuit slot. Refer to exploded view drawing on page 50.

Hinges

Step 19 - Folding hinges (R) are used to hold the lids up at an angle, making recycling much easier. Follow the directions that come with the folding hinge on how to install.

Cut the inside divider (G) to the dimensions given in the material list. Attach the divider to the front rail and rear rail using biscuits.

Cut the backing (J) to the dimensions given in the material list. Attach the backing to the sides and bottom back edges using 1" brads.

Final Assembly

Step 20 - Remove all hardware. Paint the entire assembly except for the doors, lids and base boards with the color of your choice. Finish the doors, lids and base boards with several coats of Danish Oil. Once the paint has dried, glue up the front base board and the center stile with biscuits as shown in Step 20. (Be sure the front base board is centered). Attach the side base boards. Attach the lids, doors and knobs.

End Table

Rails and Stiles

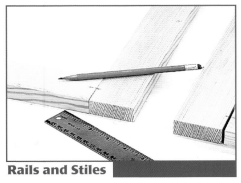

Step 1 - Tip: It's best to buy a basket first so that any necessary adjustments to the cabinet can be made.

Cut the side, back and front rails (A, C, E, F) and the side and back stiles (B, D) to the dimensions given in the material list. Lay out the frames and mark for biscuits in the center where the rails and stiles meet, as shown in Step 1.

Cut Biscuit Slots

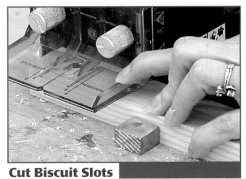

Step 2 - Cut the #R3-size biscuit slots in the stiles where marked in the previous step, using a biscuit joiner as shown in Step 2.

Rail Slots

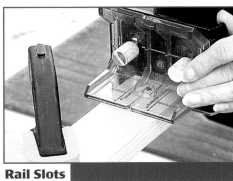

Step 3 - Cut the #R3-size slots in the ends of the rails where marked, using the biscuit joiner as shown in Step 3.

Biscuits and Glue

Step 4 - To make up the frames for the sides and the back, glue the stiles to the rails using the #R3 biscuits (M) in the slots as shown in Step 4. Clamp and let it dry.

Sand the frames through 220-grit sandpaper.

Material List				T x W x L
A side rails	(pine)	4		¾" x 2" x 22"
B side stiles	(pine)	4		¾" x 2" x 11½"
C back rails	(pine)	2		¾" x 2" x 7"
D back stiles	(pine)	2		¾" x 1¼" x 11½"
E front bottom rail	(pine)	1		¾" x 1⅝" x 9½"
F front top rail	(pine)	1		¾" x 1" x 9½"
G side panels	(beadboard)	2		¼" x 22¾" x 8⅛"
H back panel	(beadboard)	1		¼" x 7¾" x 8⅛"
I bottom	(pine)	1		¾" x 9½" x 24⅝"
J top	(oak)	1		¾" x 13" x 28"

Supply List				
K turned legs	(hardwood)	4		9"
L vertical top plates		4		
M biscuits				#R3, #0
N brads				⅝", 1¼"
O wood filler				
P rabbeting bit				¼" x ⅜"
Q chisel and mallet				
R decorative router bit				
S latex enamel paint	(your choice)			
T ZAR interior spray polyurethane (clear gloss)				
U sturdy basket with handles				7½" x 8" x 19"

Rout Rabbet

Step 5 - Put a ¼" rabbeting bit (P) in the router and rout a ¼"-deep by ⅜"-wide rabbet around the inside bottom of all the frames as shown in Step 5.

Square Corners

Step 6 - Square the corners of each rabbet using a chisel and mallet (Q) as shown in Step 6.

Cut the side and back panels (G, H) to the dimensions given in the material list.

Attach Panels

Step 7 - Using the ⅝" brads (N), attach the panels to their respective frames.

Cut the bottom (I) to the dimensions given in the material list. Mark the positions for the #0 biscuits on the bottom, referring to the side view on page 55 and the exploded drawing on page 57 for biscuit placements.

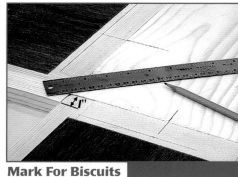

Mark For Biscuits

Step 8 - Lay the sides and back pieces flat along the bottom. The sides will overhang the bottom by ¾" along the back edge of the bottom. Continue the lines from the bottom, up the sides and back. Mark a horizontal line ⅜" from the rabbets for the sides and back biscuit locations as shown in Step 8.

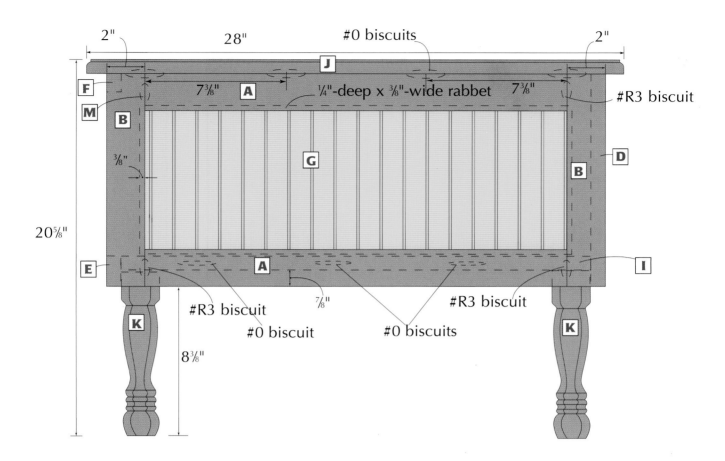

2"   28"   #0 biscuits   2"

J

F
M
B

7³⁄₈"   A   ¼"-deep x ³⁄₈"-wide rabbet   7³⁄₈"   #R3 biscuit

D

³⁄₈"   G   B

B

20⁵⁄₈"

E   A   I

#R3 biscuit   ⁷⁄₈"   #R3 biscuit

#0 biscuit   #0 biscuits

K   8³⁄₈"   K

Side View

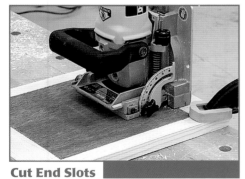

Cut End Slots

Step 9 - Cut the #0 biscuit slots where marked on the sides and back as shown in Step 9.

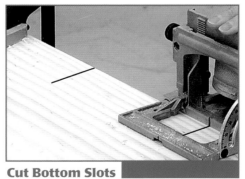

Cut Bottom Slots

Step 10 - The bottom slots are cut on the edge of the bottom where marked as shown in Step 10.

Glue and Clamp

Step 11 - Glue and biscuit the sides and back to the bottom. Glue the back panel to the sides. Clamp the back of the carcass together. Glue the front top and bottom rails in place, making sure that the top of the bottom rail is flush with the top edge of the bottom. Clamp as shown in Step 11.

Brad Rails

Step 12 - Using the 1¼" brads (N), brad the sides to the back and the front rails in place as shown in Step 12. Let the glue dry.

Pre-Drill

Step 13 - Turn the carcass over and place a vertical top plate (L) in each corner of the bottom. Use a ⅛" drill bit to pre-drill for the plate screws as shown in Step 13.

Cut the top (J) to the dimensions given in the material list.

Front View

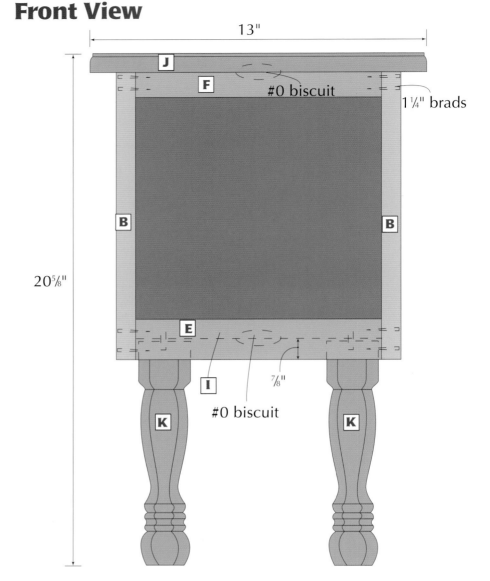

13"

20⅝"

J

F

#0 biscuit

1¼" brads

B

B

E

I

⅞"

#0 biscuit

K

K

Rout Top

Step 14 - Use the decorative router bit of your choice (R) in the router and rout around the upper edge of the top piece as shown in Step 14. Sand the top through 220-grit sandpaper.

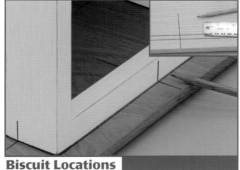

Biscuit Locations

Step 15 - For the biscuit locations along the top edge of the carcass, place the top, top side down and center the carcass on the top. Using a pencil, trace on the underneath side of the top, around the outside edge of the carcass as shown in Step 15.

Refer to the drawings on pages 55 and 56 for the top biscuit locations. Measure in ⅜" from the pencil line and mark for the biscuit slots as shown in Step 15 inset.

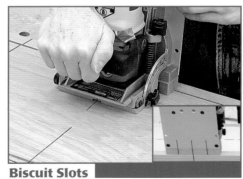

Biscuit Slots

Step 16 - Using the biscuit joiner set for the #0 biscuits, cut the slots where marked on the underneath side of the top, as shown in Step 16. Repeat these same steps with the biscuit joiner along the top edge of the carcass as shown in Step 16 inset.

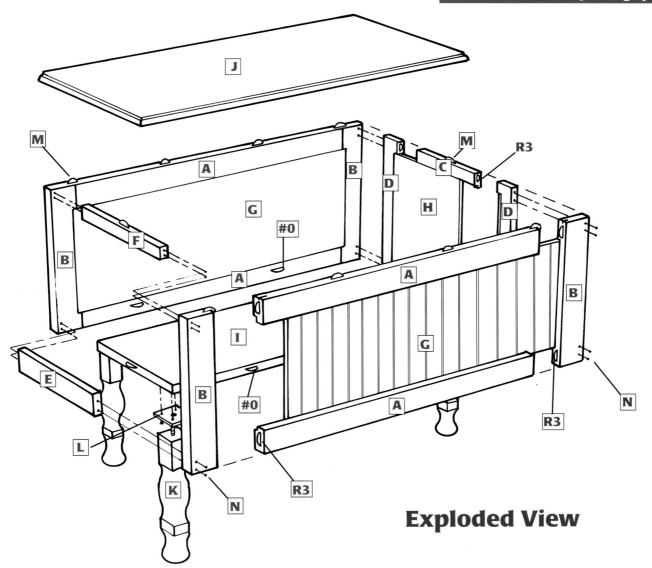

Exploded View

Finish

Step 17 - Fill any brad holes with wood filler (O). Sand pieces thoroughly through 220-grit sandpaper. Finish the end table as desired. I used a latex enamel paint (S) for the base and the legs (K) and a spray-on polyurethane (T) for the top, as shown in Step 17. Let dry completely. Sand the edges of the legs and cabinet for a worn look, if desired.

Finish

Step 18 - To attach the top, place glue in each biscuit slot and along the top edge of the base as shown in Step 18 inset. Clamp the top to the base until dry as shown in Step 18.

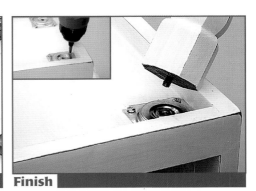

Finish

Step 19 - Install the vertical top plates where previously pre-drilled as shown in Step 19 inset. Screw on the turned legs as shown in Step 19.

Place the store-bought basket (U) into the base and enjoy.

Pop-Up Coffee Table

Two for one, that's what you get when you make this unique pop-up coffee table. Leave it down, and it's your everyday coffee table. Lift the top, and it becomes a table for those gourmet frozen dinners.

Ripping Legs

Step 1 - Cut the legs (A) to the dimensions given in material list. Use the radial arm saw with a stop block as shown in Step 1. Using a stop block will give you the exact same length for all four legs.

Mortise Layout

Step 2 - The legs receive mortises for the sides and ends (B, C). Refer to the Mortise and Tenon drawing on page 59 for mortise locations. Use a mortise tool to layout where the mortises are to go as shown in Step 2.

Mortising Jig

Step 3 - To save time, a mortising tool is used on the drill press. This tool has a drill bit inside that does most of the cutting and a four-sided chisel to square the mortise as shown in Step 3.

Material List				T x W x L
A legs	(oak	4		2½" x 2½" x 15"
B sides	(oak plywood)	2		¾" x 4" x 36½"
C ends	(oak plywood)	2		¾" x 4" x 20¼"
Panels				
D side stiles	(oak)	4		¾" x 1¼" x 5½"
E side rails	(oak)	4		¾" x 1¼" x 35"
F end stiles	(oak)	4		¾" x 1¼" x 5½"
G end rails	(oak)	4		¾" x 1¼" x 18¾"
H side bead boards		2		¼" x 6" x 33"
I end bead boards		2		¼" x 6" x 16¾"
Table Lid				
J table lid		1		¾" x 28" x 44"
K table lid side banding		2		1¼" x 2" x 48"
L table lid end banding		2		1¼" x 2" x 32"
TableTop				
M top		1		¾" x 21½" x 37¾"
Inset Box				
N sides	(oak plywood)	2		¾" x 3¼" x 20"
O bottom	(oak plywood)	1		¾" x 20" x 26½"
Supply List				
P wood screws		24		#6 x 1¼"
Q wood screws		6		#6 x 1⅜"
R biscuits		24		#10
S oak plugs		6		⅜" x ⅜"
T pop-up table mechanism*		1		#35460

*This item is available from Rockler catalog. For more information, call 800-279-4441, or visit their web site at **www.rockler.com**.

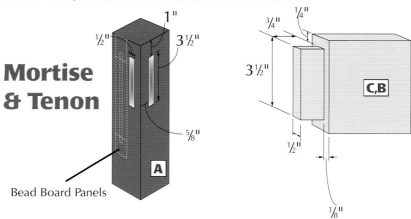

Mortise & Tenon

Bead Board Panels

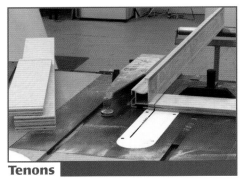

Tenons

Step 4 - Cut the sides and ends (B, C) to the dimensions given in the material list. Use the table saw to make the first cheek cut on both sides of each piece as shown in Step 4. Refer to the mortise and tenon drawing on page 59 for tenon dimensions.

Shoulder Cut

Step 5 - With the blade set to the proper height, turn the side and end pieces upright to make the shoulder cuts as shown in Step 5.

Tenoning Jig

Step 6 - To remove the cheeks from both side and end pieces, use a tenoning jig on the table saw. Raise the blade to the proper height. Set the jig so that the off-cut falls to the right of the blade as shown in Step 6. Remove the shoulder using a table saw with a miter gauge as shown in Step 6 inset.

Table Top

Step 7 - Cut the table top (M) to the dimensions given in the material list. Dry assemble the legs, sides and ends. Lay the table top down and flip the legs, sides and ends on top of the table top. Square the two together. Trace around where the inside corner of each leg meets the table top as shown in Step 7. Use a jigsaw to remove the notches as shown in Step 7 inset.

Tenon Glue-Up

Step 8 - Place the table top and leg assembly together as shown in Step 8. Glue the mortises and tenons of each leg, side and end together. The table top is not glued down; it's dry-fitted to keep the leg assembly square while gluing.

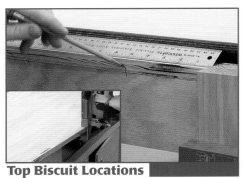

Top Biscuit Locations

Step 9 - The table top gets fastened to the sides and ends using #10 biscuits (R). Evenly space three biscuits along the sides and two biscuits along the ends as shown in Step 9. Use a biscuit joiner to make the slots in the table top, sides and ends as shown in Step 9 inset.

Top View

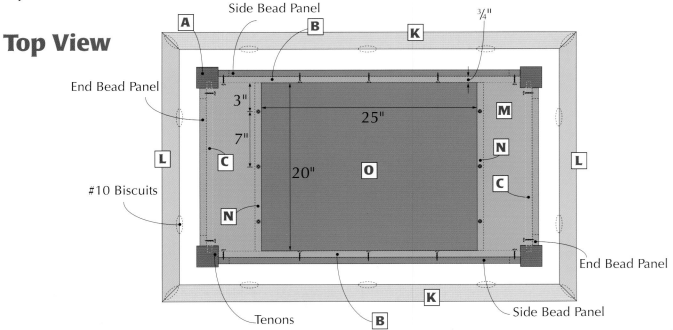

Jigsawing

Step 10 - Refer to the top view drawing on page 60 for center hole cut-out. Mark the dimensions on the table top. Use tape around the dimensions to prevent splintering. Use the jigsaw to remove the center opening as shown in Step 10.

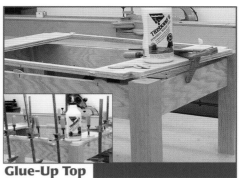

Glue-Up Top

Step 11 - With all of the biscuit slots cut into the table top, sides and ends, glue and clamp the table top to the leg assembly as shown in Step 11 and Step 11 inset. Set aside to dry.

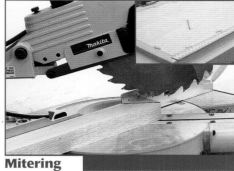

Mitering

Step 12 - Cut the table lid side bandings and end bandings (K, L) to the dimensions given in the material list. The banding will hide the end grain of the plywood. Forty-fives are cut on the ends of each banding piece. Forty-fives can be tricky; you can butt the ends together for the same effect. If you do decide to butt the ends, be sure to make the necessary adjustments in the measurements. Use the miter saw to make the forty-fives as shown in Step 12. Cut the table lid (J) to the dimensions given in the material list. Place the banding around the table lid. Evenly space four #10 biscuit locations along the sides and three along the ends as shown in Step 12 inset.

Exploded View

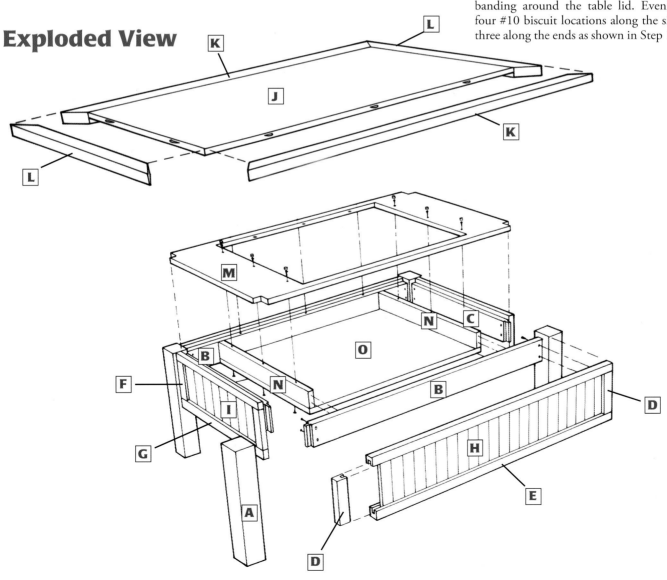

Table Lid Biscuit

Step 13 - With all of the biscuit slot locations on the table lid, use the biscuit joiner set to make #10 slots. Clamp the table lid down and mill the slots as shown in Step 13.

Banding Biscuits

Step 14 - Matching biscuit slot locations are on the side and end bandings. Be sure to place a biscuit slot in the miters if you are using forty-fives in the corners, as shown in Step 14. Repeat step for the remaining slots as shown in the Step 14 inset.

Banding Lid Glue-Up

Step 15 - Spread glue into all of the slots and around the edges of the table lid. Place biscuits in slots. Clamp the assembly together as shown in Step 15. The banding is thicker than the plywood lid; be sure to flush the top edges.

Grooves

Step 16 - Cut the side stiles, side rails, end stiles and end rails (D, E, F, G) to the dimensions given in the material list. Make ¼" x ¼" through dadoes down the inside edges of each stile and rail. Use the router table with a ¼" bit to make the dadoes as shown in Step 16. Cut the side bead boards and end bead boards (H, I) to the dimensions given in the material list. Glue and clamp the stiles and rails together with the bead boards in the center dadoes. The bead boards require no glue; they just float in the dadoes as shown in Step 16 inset.

Pre-Drilling

Step 17 - Clamp the completed side and ends panels in-between the leg assembly. Flush the panels' top edges with the table top. Pre-drill and screw through the table top into the side panels using the wood screws (P) as shown in Step 17 and Step 17 inset.

Pre-Drill

Step 18 - Stand the table upright onto its end. Pre-drill and screw the panels into place, as shown in Step 18.

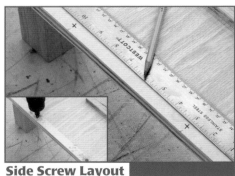

Side Screw Layout

Step 19 - Cut the sides and bottom (N, O) to the dimensions given in the material list. Refer to the top view drawing on page 60 for side screw locations. Pre-drill and countersink for the wood screws (Q).

Fasten Sides

Step 20 - Glue and screw the sides into place, as shown in Step 20. Make plugs to cover the screw heads as shown in Step 20 inset.

Fasten Bottom

Step 21 - Turn the table upside down. Place the bottom (O) onto the sides (N). Pre-drill and screw the bottom and sides into place as shown in Step 21. Add several coats of oil for the finish. Mount the pop-up mechanism (T) and lid according to the manufacturer's directions.

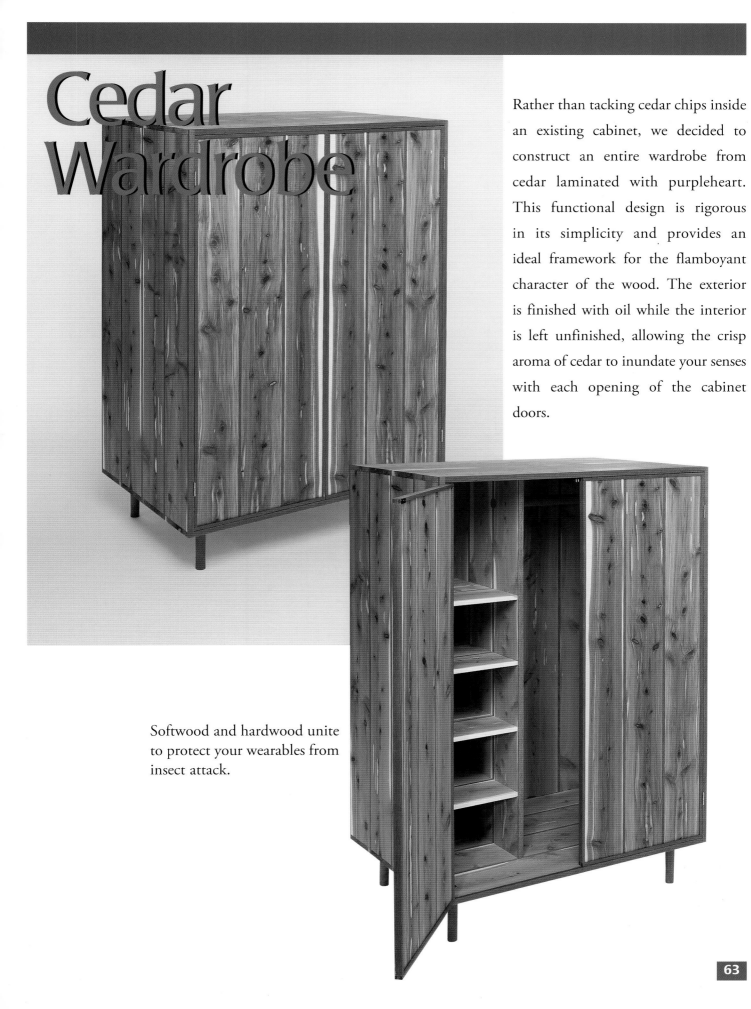

Cedar Wardrobe

Rather than tacking cedar chips inside an existing cabinet, we decided to construct an entire wardrobe from cedar laminated with purpleheart. This functional design is rigorous in its simplicity and provides an ideal framework for the flamboyant character of the wood. The exterior is finished with oil while the interior is left unfinished, allowing the crisp aroma of cedar to inundate your senses with each opening of the cabinet doors.

Softwood and hardwood unite to protect your wearables from insect attack.

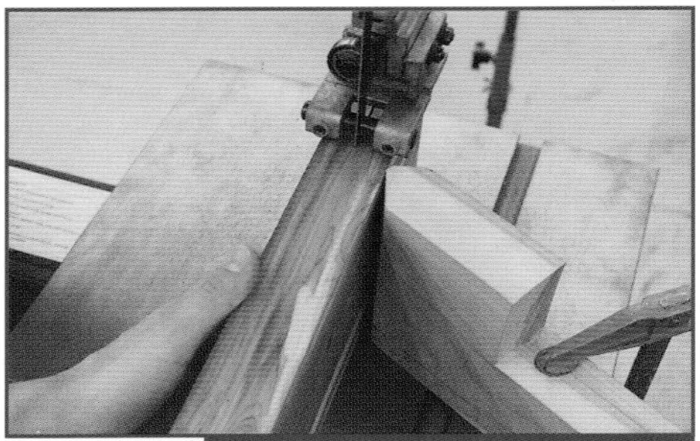

Band saw

Step 1 - This project is time consuming and is recommended for the woodworker looking for a rewarding challenge. Read through the article and study the drawings and step photos carefully before beginning. The cedar for this project came from eleven 1¾" x 5½" x 8' boards and the purpleheart from one 2" x 10"x 8' board. Cut all of the boards in half lengthwise and resaw on the band saw as shown in Step 1. Keep all of the resawn cedar paired and bookmatched during lamination.

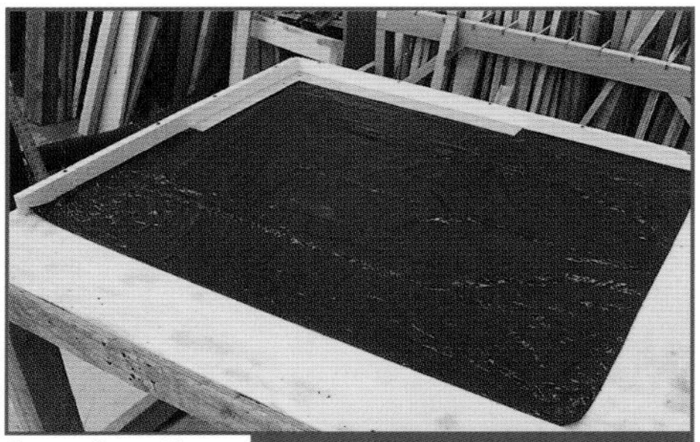

Lamination

Step 2 - On a large work table, make the laminating jig shown in Step 2. Attach plywood rails to two adjacent sides, and keep two rails loose for clamping. Lay out a large trashbag and stick it down with double-sided tape to prevent any squeeze-out from adhering to the work table. The material list gives dimensions for individual slats which are laminated together to form the sides, top, etc. Cut the members for the sides (A) and back (B) to the dimensions given in the material list. Plane down the resawn boards to ⅝" before cutting to length and save offcuts to use as spacers when laminating.

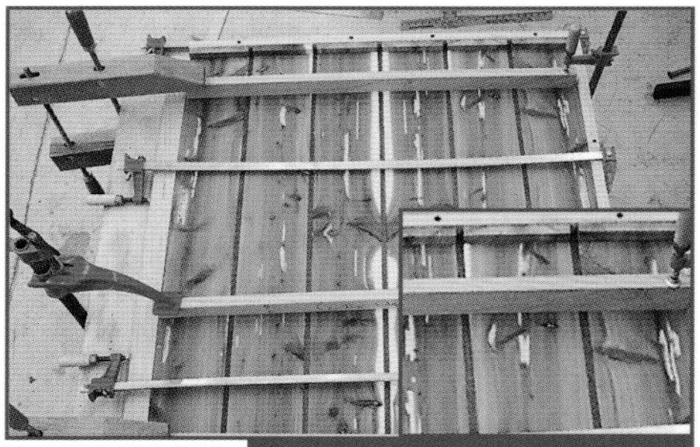

Lamination

Step 3 - Glue up the sides and back with the spacers in place as shown in Step 3.

Material List				**T x W x L**
A	sides (2)	(cedar)	8	5/8" x 5 1/4" x 44"
		(purpleheart)*	10	3/8" x 5/8" x 45 1/4"
B	back	(cedar)	6	5/8" x 5 1/4" x 44"
		(purpleheart)*	5	3/8" x 5/8" x 45 1/4"
C	top, bottom	(cedar)	8	5/8" x 5 1/4"x 34 5/8"
		(purpleheart)*	10	3/8" x 5/8" x 33 3/8"
D	divider	(cedar)	3	5/8" x 5 1/4" x 44 1/2"
		(purpleheart)*	3	3/8" x 5/8" x 44 1/2"
E	shelves (4)	(cedar)	12	1/2" x 5 1/4" x 12 1/2"
		(purpleheart)*	8	3/8" x 1/2" x 12 1/2"
F	leg blanks	(purpleheart)*	2	2" x 2" x 15 1/4"
G	door panels (2)	(cedar)	6	3/8" x 5 1/8" x 43 1/2"
		(purpleheart)*	4	3/8" x 3/8" x 43 1/2"
H	door stiles	(purpleheart)*	4	3/8" x 3/4" x 43 7/8"
I	door rails	(purpleheart)*	4	3/8" x 3/4" x 16 5/8"
J	clothes pole	(teak)	1	1 1/4" diam. x 25"
Supply List				
K	magnetic touch latch (double)**			
L	brass hinges		4	1 1/2"

*Note—any hardwood can be substituted for purpleheart.
**Hardware available through Woodworker's Supply 800-645-9292.

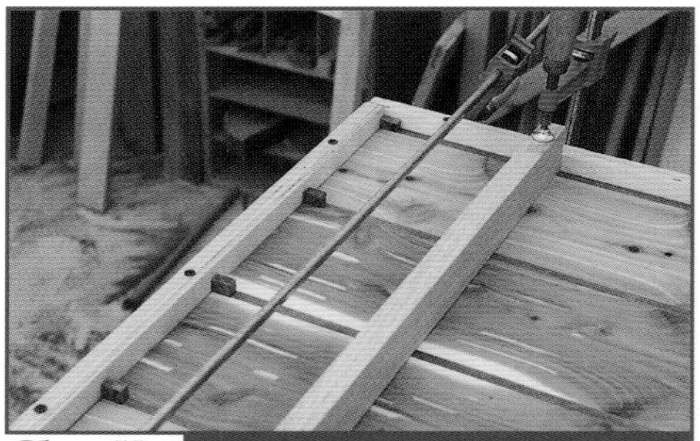

Glue-Up

Step 4 - Cut the members for the top and bottom (C) and glue-up using the purpleheart offcuts for spacers as shown in Step 4. The divider (D) and shelves (E) are laminated using the same process, but no spacers are needed since the end members are flush. Cut the members to the dimensions given in the material list, and glue-up on the work table.

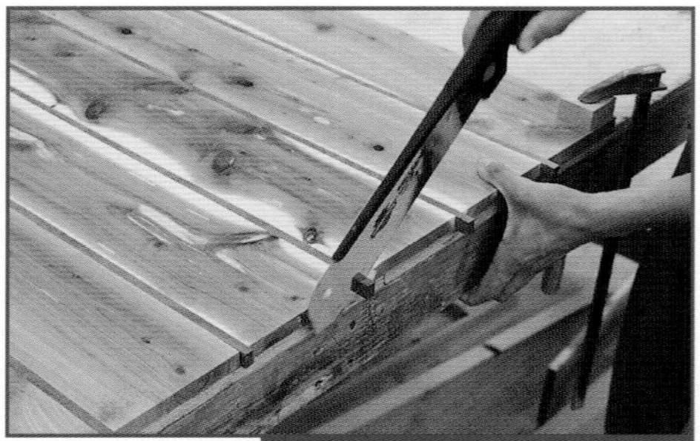

Back Tenons

Step 5 - Saw the tenons on the back to a length of ¼" as shown in Step 5.

Chisel Tenons

Step 6 - Chisel the tenons to a thickness of ¼" as shown in Step 6. These tenons allow the back to float in the cabinet once the case is glued up.

Dadoes

Step 7 - Cut the dadoes that will receive the divider into the top and bottom using the router with a ⅜" straight bit set to a depth of ¼" as shown in Step 7.

Clamp

Step 8 - Clamp a fence to the work to guide the cut. Refer to the drawings for dado locations. Cut the dadoes that will receive the shelves into the divider and side using the router with a ½" straight bit set to a depth of ¼." Chisel square all stopped dadoes as shown in Step 8.

Mortises

Step 9 - Mortises in the top and bottom receive the tenons on the top and bottom edges of the back. Place a mark at each location where the tenons in the back will make contact with the top and bottom. Center 1" mortises at each of these points ⅜" in from the outside edge, as shown in the exploded detail. Cut the mortises using the router with a ¼" straight bit set to a depth of ⁵⁄₁₆" as shown in Step 9.

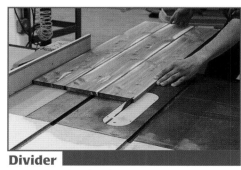

Divider

Step 10 - The divider, as is, will not fit into the dadoes in the top and bottom. Cut the divider to a width of 16⅜," making the cut along the back edge as shown in Step 10.

Back/Leg Detail

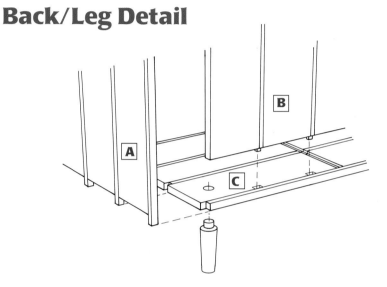

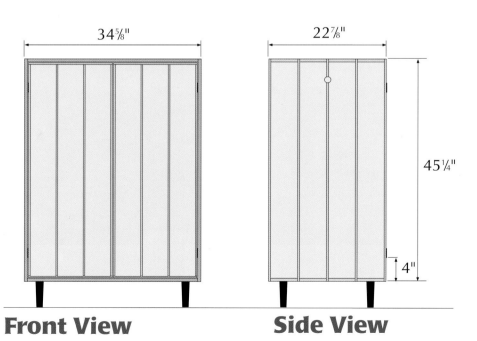

34⅝"

22⅞"

45¼"

4"

Front View

Side View

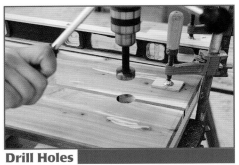

Drill Holes

Step 11 - Mark the holes for the clothes pole on the divider and side without dadoes as located in the drawings. Drill the holes using a 1¼" Forstner bit on the drill press as shown in Step 11. Clamp the work firmly and use a backing block to prevent tear out.

Shelf/Divider Detail

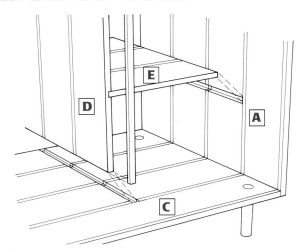

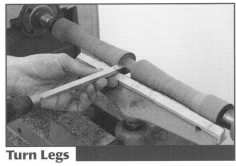

Turn Legs

Step 12 - Cut the leg blanks (F) to the dimensions given in the material list. (Each blank yields two legs.) Turn each blank on the lathe as shown in Step 12, forming the ⅞"-diameter tenon for each leg in the center of the blank. Make the center section wide enough to allow for the kerf of a blade when you cut the turned work into two legs, each with ⅜"-long tenons.

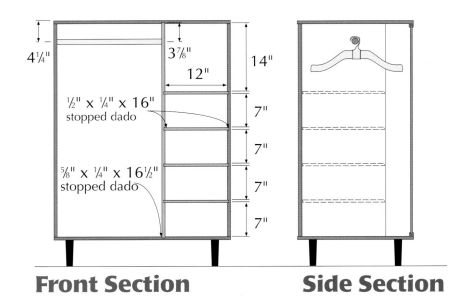

Front Section

Side Section

Drill Press

Step 13 - Mortises secure the leg tenons to the bottom. Measure 3" in from each edge at each of the four corners of the bottom to find the centerpoint for the mortises. Use a ⅞" Forstner bit on the drill press to make the mortises. Clamp the work securely and use a backing block as shown in Step 13.

Glue-Up Legs

Step 14 - Test fit each of the four legs, and glue-up two legs at a time as shown in Step 14. If some of the tenons fit too loosely, wrap medical gauze tightly around the tenon and soak with plenty of glue.

Glue-Up Case

Step 15 - Test fit all joints and file down any obstructing areas. Glue-up the case, two laminated boards at a time, using the work table and stationary glue-up jig from previous laminations. Start with the top and side that contains shelf dadoes, making at least one dry run with all the clamps applied. Once you feel comfortable with the procedure, apply glue and clamp as shown in Step 15.

Glue-Up Case

Step 16 - Once glue has dried, rotate the assembly 180 degrees so that the bottom and opposite side can be clamped against the stationary jig as before. Lay the back on the work table and test fit the entire cabinet with the shelves and divider in place, applying all clamps in a dry run. When ready, apply glue and clamps. Let the back float and apply a dab of glue only to the front of the stopped dadoes as shown in Step 16. This will allow the interior of the cabinet to expand and contract. Check for square. Once glue is dry, have a friend help you lift the assembly off of the work table and onto the floor.

Clothes Pole

Step 17 - Slide the clothes pole blank (J) into the pre-drilled holes in the side and divider and mark the length with a pencil. Cut the clothes pole to size as shown in Step 17. Glue-up the clothes pole in the cabinet and sand it flush with the side when dry. Sand the entire cabinet through 150-grit sandpaper.

Doors

Step 18 - Cut the door panels (G) to the dimensions given in the material list. Glue-up the panels using the stationary jig on the work table. While the glue is drying, cut the purpleheart door stiles (H) and door rails (I) to the dimensions given in the material list. Finger joints connect the stiles to the rails. Mark and cut the fingers using the table saw with a miter gauge and the blade set to a depth of ⅜" as shown in Step 18. Clear out any waste between fingers after the initial cuts have been made.

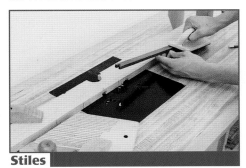

Stiles

Step 19 - Cut stopped and through dadoes into the stiles and rails on the router table using a ⅜" straight bit set to a depth of 3/16" as shown in Step 19.

Chisel Dado Ends

Step 20 - Chisel square all of the dado ends as shown in Step 20. Sand all frame members and door panels through 150-grit sandpaper before gluing up the frame.

Glue-Up Frame

Step 21 - If everything fits properly and is square, glue up the frame with the panel in place as shown in Step 21. Repeat for the other door.

Hanging Doors

Step 22 - Mark the hinge (L) mortise on the cabinet as located in the drawing. Make a measuring block to ensure all hinge locations are identical.

Mark Location

Step 23 - Mark the corresponding location for the hinge on the doors as shown in Step 23.

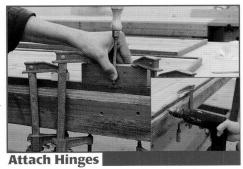

Attach Hinges

Step 24 - Chisel the mortises. Mark the screw locations, drill pilot holes and attach hinges to the doors before securing in the cabinet. Have a friend help you hang the doors in the cabinet. Attach a double magnetic touch latch (K) to the inside top of the cabinet, making sure the doors close flush with the front edge. Attach the magnetic plates to the corresponding location on each door. Finish the exterior of the wardrobe with two coats of oil and a final coat of wax.

Cherry Valet

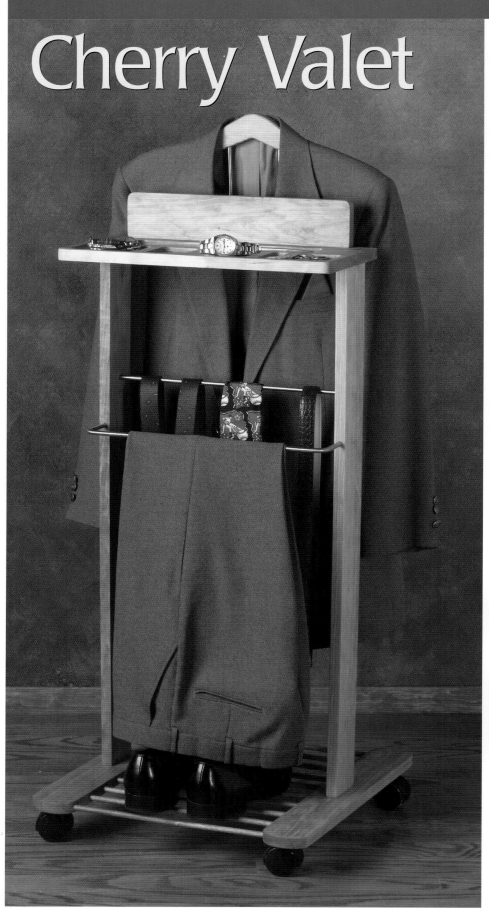

Dimensioning

Step 1 - Cut the feet (A), legs (B), top shelf (C) and back splash (D) to the dimensions given in the material list. Use the radial arm saw to cut the lengths and the table saw to cut the widths as shown in Step 1.

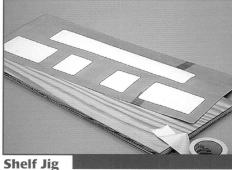

Shelf Jig

Step 2 - Cut the shelf jig (H) to the dimensions given in the material list. Locate the top shelf halved jig pattern. Make a photocopy and adhere it to the jig blank with double-sided tape as shown in Step 2.

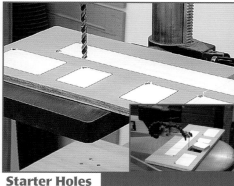

Starter Holes

Step 3 - Use the drill press with a ¼" drill bit to drill starter holes in each of the white portions of the jig pattern as shown in Step 3.

Use the scroll saw to remove the white portions of the pattern as shown in Step 3 inset.

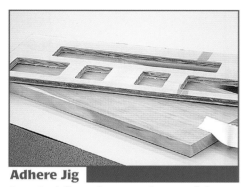

Adhere Jig

Step 4 - Adhere the jig to the top of the top shelf with double-sided tape as shown in Step 4.

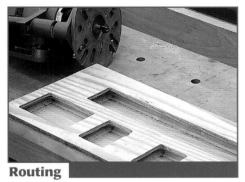

Routing

Step 5 - Use the router with a ½"-wide by ¾"-long cove bit and a ¼" collar installed in the router to make the five indentations on the top shelf. Remove just a little material with each pass until you reach a depth of ⅜" as shown in Step 5.

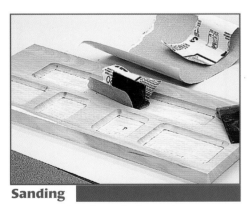

Sanding

Step 6 - Hand sand the indentations to smooth out the unevenness left behind by the router bit. Use some contoured sanding pads to help as shown in Step 6.

Material List			T x W x L
A feet*	(cherry)	2	¾" x 3" x 20"
B legs	(cherry)	2	¾" x 3" x 35"
C top shelf	(cherry)	1	¾" x 8" x 18"
D back splash	(cherry)	1	¾" x 3" x 15"
E hanger*	(cherry)	1	¾" x 5" x 17"
F bottom dowels	(cherry)	10	⅜" diam. x 14"
G plugs	(cherry)	6	⅜" diam. x ⅜"
H shelf jig*	(plywood)	1	¾" x 8" x 18"
Supply List			
I twin wheel casters		4	2"
J wood screws		17	#6 x 2"
K wood screws		16	#6 x ½"
L pant bar	(stainless steel)	1	⁵⁄₁₆" diam. x 24"
M tie/belt bar	(stainless steel)	1	⁵⁄₁₆" diam. x 15¾"
N hanger bars	(stainless steel)	2	⁵⁄₁₆" diam. x 7"
O wood glue			
P two-part adhesive			
Q double-sided tape			
R Watco Danish Oil			

*See Pattern Packet.

Top View

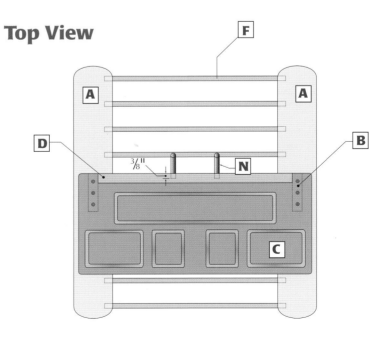

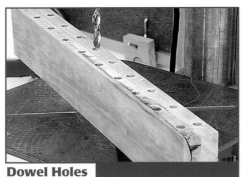

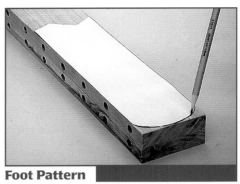

Dowel Locations

Step 7 - Gang the two feet together. Lay out the dowel hole locations on the inside edge of each foot. Start the layouts by measuring in 1" from the ends, centered and every 2" thereafter as shown in Step 7. Use an awl to start each dowel location.

Dowel Holes

Step 8 - Use the drill press with a ⅜" bit to drill each dowel location in each foot to a depth of ⅜" as shown in Step 8.

Foot Pattern

Step 9 - Locate the halved foot pattern in the pattern packet. Trace the pattern to both ends on the ganged feet as shown in Step 9.

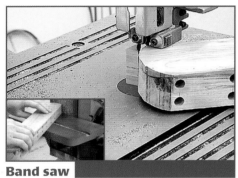

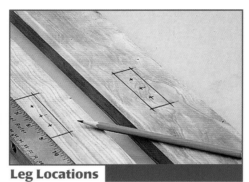

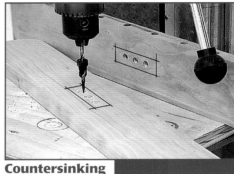

Band saw

Step 10 - Use the band saw and stationary sander to round the corners of the feet as shown in Step 10 and Step 10 inset.

Leg Locations

Step 11 - Separate the two feet. Locate the center on both feet. Lay out the leg locations on the bottom side of each foot. Each leg is 3"-wide by ¾"-thick.

Use a ruler and straight edge to show each layout. Locate three evenly spaced screw holes within the leg layout as shown in Step 11.

Countersinking

Step 12 - Use the drill press with a #6 countersink bit to pre-drill each screw location in the feet. Countersink just enough for the screw heads to sit flush as shown in Step 12.

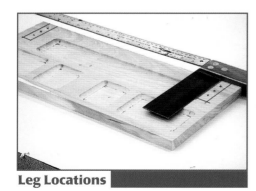

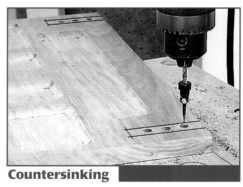

Leg Locations

Step 13 - The top shelf is mounted to the legs with the 2" wood screws (J). Lay out each leg location on the top shelf. Refer to the front, side and top view drawings for leg locations. Transfer each location as shown in Step 13.

Back Splash Location

Step 14 - The back splash (D) is mounted to the top shelf with five evenly spaced 2" wood screws (J). Lay out the back splash on the bottom side of the top shelf, centered along the shelf's back edge as shown in Step 14.

Countersinking

Step 15 - Use the drill press with the #6 countersink bit to pre-drill into the top shelf where the legs are located. Drill to a depth that allows for the wood plugs (G) as shown in Step 15.

Pre-Drilling

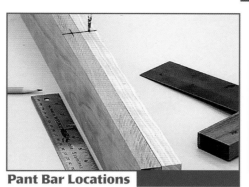

Pant Bar Locations

Tie/Belt Bar Locations

Step 16 - Flip the top shelf over and pre-drill, using the #6 countersink bit, the five screw locations for the back splash. Drill to a depth that allows the screw heads to sit flush as shown in Step 16.

Step 17 - The legs have holes drilled into them to hold the pant bar (L) and the tie/belt bar (M). For the pant bar, place the two legs together on end and measure down from the top 11½" and mark a center hole location into each leg as shown in Step 17.

Step 18 - Measure down from the top of the legs 8½". Center and mark the tie/belt bar locations on the inside of each leg as shown in Step 18.

Front View   # Side View

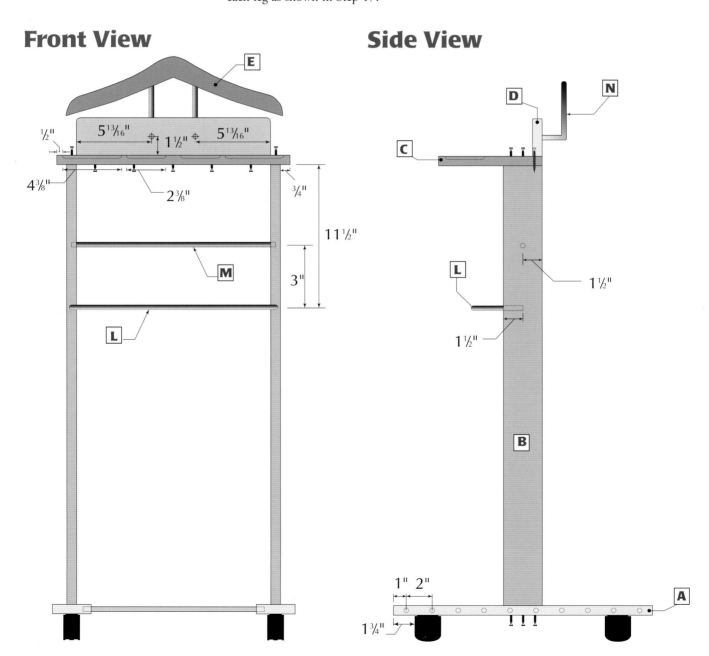

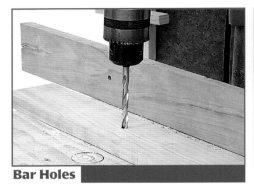

Bar Holes

Step 19 - Use the drill press with a ⁵⁄₁₆" bit to drill the stopped holes a depth of 1½" on the front edge. Turn the legs on their sides and drill to a depth of ⅜" for the tie/belt bar as shown in Step 19.

Stationary Sander

Step 20 - Cut the tie/belt bar (M) to the dimensions given in the material list.

Use the stationary sander to knock off the front corners of the top shelf and the top corners of the back splash as shown in Step 20.

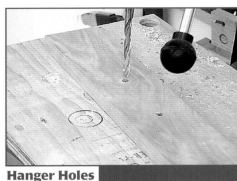

Hanger Holes

Step 21 - The back splash gets two ⁵⁄₁₆" stopped holes drilled into its back side. Refer to the front view drawing for hole locations. Mark the locations and use the drill press to drill each hole to a depth of ⅜" as shown in Step 21.

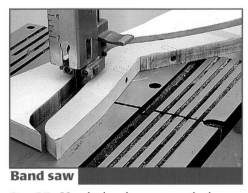

Plug Cutting

Step 22 - Sand the entire project through 220-grit sandpaper.

Cut the bottom dowels (F) to the dimensions given in the material list. Cut the plugs (G) out of a scrap piece of cherry. Use the drill press and a ⅜" plug cutting bit as shown in Step 22.

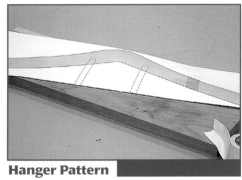

Hanger Pattern

Step 23 - Cut the hanger (E) to the dimensions given in the material list. Locate the hanger pattern and adhere it to the hanger blank as shown in Step 23.

Hanger Bar Holes

Step 24 - Located on the pattern are the hole locations for the hanger bars. Use the drill press with a ⁵⁄₁₆" drill bit to drill the two stopped holes as shown in the Step 24.

Band saw

Step 25 - Use the band saw to cut the hanger profile out as shown in Step 25.

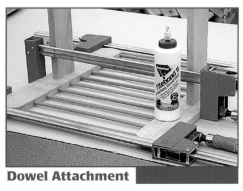

Feet Attachment

Step 26 - Attach the feet to the legs with the 2" wood screws. Use the work bench vise to hold the leg and place the foot on top of the bottom end of the leg. Pre-drill each screw location. Screw into position as shown in Step 26.

Dowel Attachment

Step 27 - Glue the bottom dowels to one foot and leg assembly. Place the tie/belt bar in position and glue the bottom dowels to the opposite foot and leg assembly. Use clamps to squeeze the dowels into place as shown in Step 27.

Shelf Attachment

Step 28 - Place the top shelf onto the legs. Flush the back edge of the legs with the back edge of the shelf. Center the shelf. Pre-drill through the holes in the shelf into the legs. Use the 2" wood screws to fasten it in place as shown in Step 28.

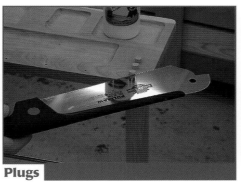

Plugs

Step 29 - To cover the screw heads on the top shelf, use some wood glue in the countersunk holes. Use a mallet to sink each plug. Use a handsaw to cut plugs flush as shown in Step 29.

Back Splash Attachment

Step 30 - Fasten the back splash (D) to the top shelf with the 2" wood screws. Clamp the back splash in place and pre-drill each hole. Screw the back splash into position as shown in Step 30.

Pant Bar

Step 31 - Cut the pant bar (L) to the dimensions given in the material list. Carefully measure the distance between the two front holes on the legs. Bend the bar with a vise to match the measurement just taken as shown in Step 31.

Pant Bar Attachment

Step 32 - Use some clamps to help draw the pant bar into place as shown in Step 32. If the bar fits loosely in the holes, use two-part adhesive (P) to hold it in place.

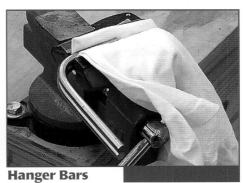

Hanger Bars

Step 33 - Cut the two hanger bars (N) to the dimensions given in the material list. Use a vise to put a 90-degree bend in each piece, starting the bend 2½" in from one end. If possible, bend both bars at the same time to assure the same lengths as shown in Step 33. Use a long pipe as a cheater bar to help make the bend.

Rounding Over

Step 34 - Use the router with a ¼" round-over bit to ease the edges of the hanger (E). Round over both edges as shown in Step 34.

Use two-part adhesive to hold the hanger bars in place. Place some adhesive in both the back splash and hanger.

Wheel Attachment

Step 35 - Finish the project with several coats of Watco Danish Oil (R).

Attach the wheel casters (I) to the feet. Measure in 1¾" from the edges for the wheel locations as shown in Step 35.

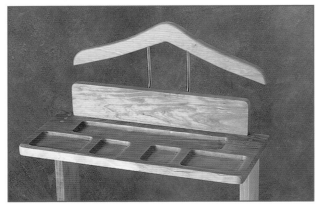

Front View

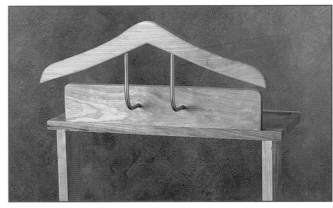

Back View

Exploded View

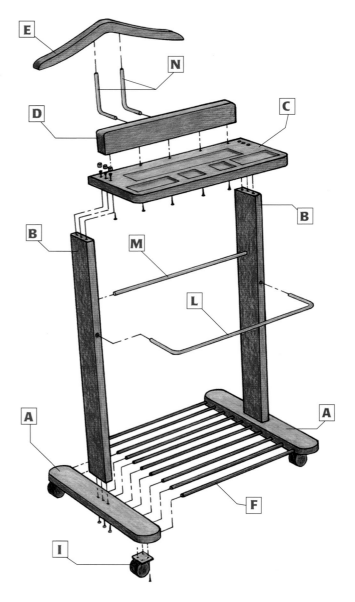

Personalized Toy Box

We show this as a toy box, but with such a nice finish you could easily turn this project into a hope chest.

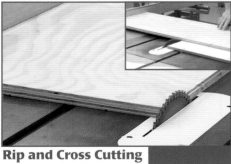

Rip and Cross Cutting

Step 1 - Cut the box pieces (A–D) to the dimensions given in the material list. Use the fence on the table saw to cut the widths as shown in Step 1. Use the sliding miter table to cut lengths as shown in Step 1 inset.

Banding

Step 2 - Cut the box banding pieces (K–M) to the dimensions given in the material list. Use the table saw with the fence and push stick for safety as shown in Step 2.

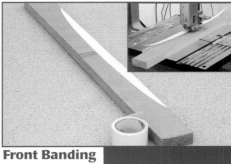

Front Banding

Step 3 - Locate the pattern and adhere it to the face side of the front banding as shown in Step 3. Use the band saw to cut the profile out as shown in Step 3 inset.

Sanding and Routing

Step 4 - To remove the rough cut on the front banding profile, use the drill press with a drum sander to sand smooth to the line on the pattern as shown in Step 4. On the face side of the front banding, round over the curved section with a router and a ¼" round-over bit as shown in Step 4 inset.

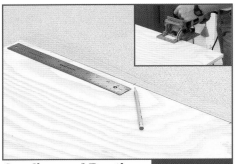

Sanding and Routing

Step 5 - Biscuits (T) are used to connect the banding to the box pieces. Refer to the drawings on page 78 for biscuit locations. Lay out the locations on each piece as shown in Step 5. Use the biscuit joiner set to #20 to make all of the slots in the banding and the box pieces as shown in Step 5 inset.

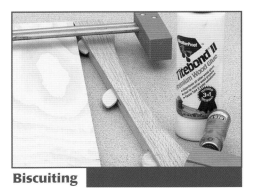

Biscuiting

Step 6 - Clamps are used to hold the banding and box pieces together while the glue sets. Spread glue into every biscuit slot and around the joining edges of the box pieces and banding pieces. Clamp all of the pieces together as shown in Step 6. Set aside to cure.

Material List			**T x W x L**
Box			
A front	(plywood)	1	¾" x 16" x 24"
B sides	(plywood)	2	¾" x 16" x 16"
C back	(plywood)	1	¾" x 16" x 24"
D bottom	(plywood)	1	¾" x 16" x 23¼"
Lid			
E lid	(oak bead board)	1	¼" x 16¼" x 23¼"
F ends*	(oak)	2	¾" x 3" x 16"
G front rail	(oak)	1	¾" x 1¾" x 24"
H back rail	(oak)	1	¾" x 1¾" x 24"
I center support bracket*	(oak)	1	¾" x 2" x 15¼"
J lid support block	(oak)	1	¾" x 1¾" x 2"
Box			
K front banding*	(oak)	1	¾" x 2" x 24"
L back banding	(oak)	1	¾" x 2" x 24"
M side banding	(oak)	2	¾" x 2" x 16"
Optional			
N block faces	(oak)	2	¾" x 4" x 4"
O lettering*	(oak)	2	¾" x 2¼" x 2½"
Supply List			
P piano hinge		1	1½" x 24"
Q friction lid support			1 National hardware
R brass wood screws			#6 x ¾"
S wood screws		16	#6 x ⅝"
T biscuits		10	#20
U caster wheels		4	
V Minwax wood sheen		1	windsor oak
W touch-up stick			oak
X vinyl pads		2	small transparent
Y brads			1"

*See Pattern Packet.

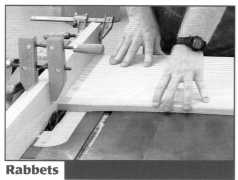

Rabbets

Step 7 - The front, back and sides are joined together at the corners with rabbets. Use a sacrificial fence and a stacked dado blade to make the ¾"-wide by ⅜"-deep through rabbets along the two inside vertical edges of the front and back pieces of the box as shown in Step 7.

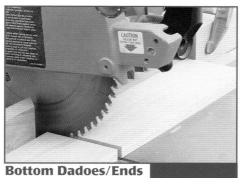

Bottom Dadoes/Ends

Step 8 - The bottom (D) of the box sits in dadoes milled into each box piece. Set the fence away 1¼" from the ¾" dado blade. Run the sides, front and back inside bottom edge through the blade. Refer to drawings on page 78.

Cut the lid ends (F) to the dimensions given in the material list as shown in Step 8.

Sawing & Sanding

Step 9 - Gang the two ends together using double-sided tape. Cut the lid end profiles out using the band saw as shown in Step 9. Use the drill press with a drum sander attached to sand smooth any saw marks left behind by the band saw as shown in Step 9 inset.

Routing Groove

Step 10 - The lid ends receive grooves along their inside top edges. Use a fence set back ½" from the ¼" straight cutting bit. Adjust the height to ⅜." When pushing the ends through the bit, be sure to keep it up against the fence as shown in Step 10.

20-Degree Rip

Step 11 - The front and back rails (G–H) receive 20-degree angles cut on their long horizontal edges. Adjust the fence away from the bottom edge of the tilted blade to 1⅜". Run each rail through to achieve the proper width as shown in Step 11. Cut each rail to length.

Rail Grooves

Step 12 - Each rail receives a dado to help hold the lid in place. Use the table saw with a ¼" dado blade tilted to 20 degrees and raised to ⅜" to make the dadoes on the inside edge of each rail. Set the fence away from the bottom edge of the dado blade to ⅞" as shown in step 12.

Rail Rabbets

Step 13 - The rails' inside ends are rabbeted for the lid ends (F). Move the fence back and away from the blade ¾." Raise the blade to ⅜." With the miter gauge, pass one edge through the blade to make the shoulder cut. Nibble away at the remaining material as shown in Step 13. Repeat these steps for the remaining edges.

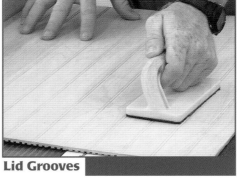

Lid Grooves

Step 14 - Cut the lid (E) to the dimensions given in the material list. To make the lid curve and fit into the grooves on the ends and rails, a series of kerf cuts are made to the inside. Raise the blade to ⅛" and measure in ¼" from one end. With the fence adjusted, run the lid across the blade using a safety paddle to hold the lid over the blade as shown in Step 14. Continue to make kerf cuts across the lid, skipping every ¼" or so.

Lid and Box Assembly

Step 15 - The rails and ends are fastened to each other using 1" brads (Y). Place glue inside the rabbets on the rails. Slide the lid into the grooves, no glue. Clamp the rails and ends and fasten them using the brad gun as shown in Step 15. Place glue into the rabbets on the front and back pieces of the box. Place the bottom piece into the dadoes. Clamp the box together and fasten along the rabbets with 1" brads. Fasten it to the bottom with 1" brads.

Hinge Assembly

Step 16 - Cut the piano hinge (P) to the length given in the material list. Place the hinge on the back edge of the box. Use an awl to mark each screw location as shown in Step 16.

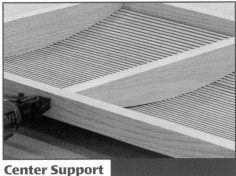

Center Support

Step 17 - Cut the center support (I) to the dimensions given in the material list. Locate the pattern and adhere it with double-sided tape. Band saw out the profile; sand through 220-grit sandpaper. Locate the center of the lid. Fasten the center support to the lid using 1" brads as shown in Step 17.

Assembly

Step 18 - Hold the lid in the open position and mark for the hinge. Pre-drill and fasten the hinge to the box and lid using the brass screws (R) as shown in Step 18.

Step 19 - Mark the locations and attach the wheels (U) to the bottom using the wood screws (S).

Step 20 - Add pre-made decorative touches as desired.

Step 21 - The lid, banding and inside box was finished with the Minwax stain (V). The outer box was painted to look antiqued. Vinyl (X) pads where placed on the lid. A friction hinge (Q) was placed inside with a block (J) attached to the end piece on the lid.

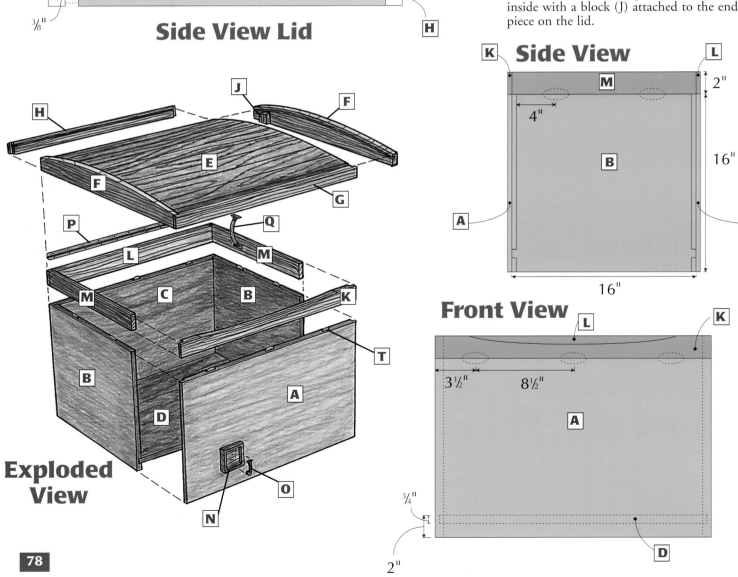

Side View Lid

Exploded View

Side View

Front View

Aces High

Call the guys, break out the snacks...

...and that's just the beginning of the fun! This walnut and oak poker chip carousel is a classic. It holds 400 poker chips and two decks of cards. So before the next guys' night out, go to the workshop and get busy!

Laminate

Step 1 - From the dimensions given in the material list, laminate wood blanks for the sides (A) and center block (D). For the center block, an oak piece is placed between two walnut pieces.

Side Blocks

Step 2 - With a radial arm saw, cut the side blocks (A) to the dimensions given in the material list.

Measure the placements for the chip slots according to drawing on page 81.

Forstner

Step 3 - Clamp the side block (A) tightly to the drill press. Use a 1⅜" Forstner bit with an extension to drill the chip slots. Raise the table as necessary to drill completely through the block. Repeat this step for all four sides.

Bottom Block

Step 4 - Cut the bottom (B) and the inside block (C) to the dimensions given in the material list. Center the inside block on the bottom piece and glue. Countersink and screw them together using wood screws (H) as shown above.

Biscuit Joining

Step 5 - Using a biscuit joiner, cut slots for biscuits (I) where indicated in the exploded drawing on this page.

Assemble Sides

Step 6 - Place side blocks around the inside block on the bottom. Glue the biscuits into the biscuit slots, making sure to put glue on the side surfaces. Clamp together tightly until dry. Wipe off any excess glue with a damp sponge.

Material List — T x W x L

				T x W x L
A	sides	(walnut)	4	2" x 4½" x 6½"
B	bottom	(walnut)	1	¾" x 6½" x 6½"
C	inside block	(walnut)	1	2⅞" x 3⅛" x 4½"
D	center block	(oak and walnut)	1	3" x 4½" x 4½"
E	card stops	(walnut)	4	½" x ¾" x 3⅛"
F	base	(oak)	1	¾" x 7½" x 7½"
G	card suit cut-out blanks*	(oak)	4	¼" x 4" x 4"

Supply List

H	wood screws		4	#6 x 1⅝"
I	wood biscuits		4	#10
J	threaded pipe**	#018	1	⅜" diam. x 5½"
K	knurled nut**	#P431	1	¾"
L	brass loop**	#738	1	1½"
M	lazy susan		1	4"
N	wood screws		8	#6 x ½"

* See Pattern Packet.
** This item can be found in Lamp Specialties catalog #EL1. To order, call 800-225-5526 or email: sales@lamp-specialties.com. Their website is www.lamp-specialties.com.

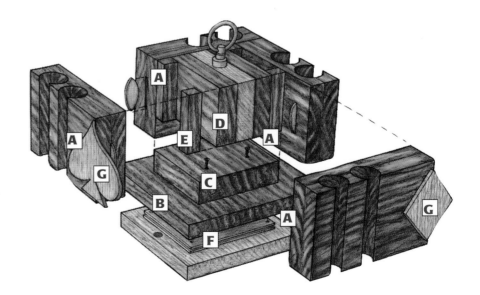

Glue and Clamp

Step 7 - Cut the laminated center block (D) to the dimensions given in the material list. Glue in place, referring to the exploded drawing on page 80. Glue the card stops (E) in each corner to help hold the center in place. Let dry completely.

Drill Center Hole

Step 8 - Find the center of the bottom and use a 1" Forstner bit to drill down ½" for the knurled nut. From the top, center and drill a ²⁵⁄₆₄" hole all the way through the project for the threaded pipe.

Round Over

Step 9 - Sand the project through 220-grit sandpaper. Cut the pipe (J) to the length given in the material list. Insert the pipe through the center and tighten, using the knurled nut (K) on the bottom. Screw the brass loop (L) to the top of the pipe.

Cut the base (F) to the dimensions given in the material list. Rout the upper edges using a ½" round-over bit, as shown in Step 9.

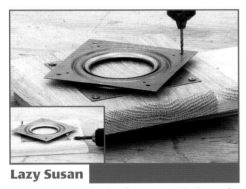

Lazy Susan

Step 10 - Attach the lazy susan (M) to the base with screws (N), making sure to center. Turn the top plate 45 degrees and with a ⅛" drill bit, drill ¼" down to mark hole.

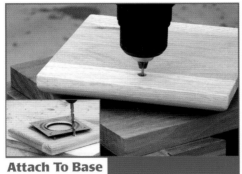

Attach To Base

Step 11 - Turn the top plate to the side and use a ³⁄₃₂" drill bit to drill through the base. See the inset on Step 11.

Turn the project over. Place a wood screw through the drilled hole and line it up with the hole in the lazy susan as shown in Step 11. Tighten the screw, and repeat these steps for the next three corners.

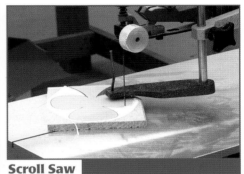

Scroll Saw

Step 12 - Tape the suit patterns on the blanks (G), using double-sided tape. Cut the profiles out on the scroll saw as shown in Step 12. Glue the shapes to the sides of the carousel and finish sanding through 220-grit sandpaper.

Finish

Step 10 - Finish with several coats of Watco Danish Oil. Now call the guys!

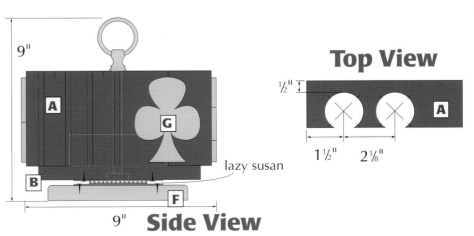

9"

A

G

B

F

lazy susan

9" **Side View**

Top View

½"

A

A

1½" 2⅛"

Potting Table

This spring, build the one you love a redwood potting table. Our version of the gardener's delight includes a built-in five-gallon sink with removable containers and a lid that functions as a watering tray and a soil sifter.

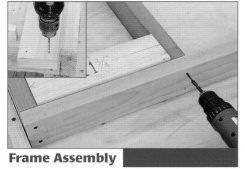

Frame Assembly

Step 1 - The potting table is made from kiln-dried redwood, available at most lumber yards. Cut the front legs (A), back legs (B), rails (C) and stretchers (D) to the dimensions given in the material list. (These members are cut from nominally dimensioned 2x4s.)

The platforms for each table top are assembled first; then the legs are attached to complete the entire table frame. Pre-drill the screw holes in the rails as located in the drawings; then screw the rails to the stretchers using #8 x 3" screws as shown in Step 1.

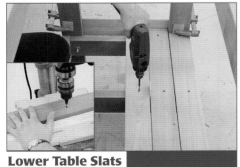

Upper Table Top Assembly

Step 2 - When assembling the upper table top, do not attach the second and third stretchers from the right in Step 4. These will be attached later after the sink hole has been cut into the table slats.

Pre-drill the holes for the lag bolts and screws into the front and back legs as shown in the inset photo in Step 2. Assemble the frame (minus the rail for the top shelf) as shown in Step 2.

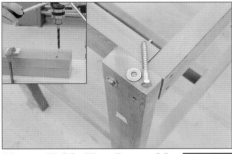

Lower Table Slats

Step 3 - Cut the full-length slats (E) and the butted slats (F) to the dimensions given in the material list. (These members are cut from nominally dimensioned 1x4s.) Pre-drill each slat, as shown in the inset photo. Screw a butted slat down along the front edge of the lower table top and continue toward the back using ⅛" spacers as shown.

Material List		T x W x L
Structure		
A front legs	2	1½" x 3½" x 37"
B back legs	2	1½" x 3½" x 50"
C rails	5	1½" x 3½" x 45"
D stretchers	9	1½" x 3½" x 18⅝"
Table top (upper and lower)		
E full-length slats	9	¾" x 3½" x 48"
F butted slats	3	¾" x 3½" x 45"
Shelf		
G top shelf	1	¾" x 6½" x 45"
Sink Lid		
H lid ends	2	1¼" x 2¾" x 12⅛"
I lid sides	2	1¼" x 2¾" x 14¾
Supply List		
J structure screws	32	#8 x 3" Grabber™
K table/shelf screws	71	#7 x 2" Grabber™
L lag screws	12	⅜" diam. x 3½"
M bolts	8	⅜" diam. x 4"
N ⅜" washers	28	⅜" diam.
O nuts	8	⅜" diam.
P ½" wire mesh	1	12" x 18"
Q ⁵⁄₁₆" washers	8	⅝" outside diam.
R Rubbermaid™ 5-gal. container		

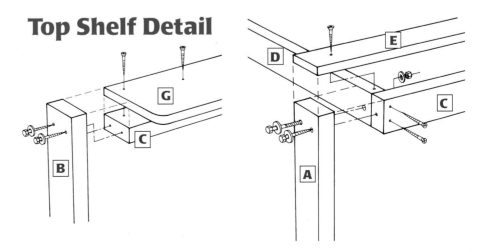

Top Shelf Detail

Table Top/Front Leg Detail

Upper Table Slats

Step 4 - Do the same for the upper table top as shown in Step 4, but do not fully tighten the screws. You will be removing the slats to make the final cuts once you have traced the shape of the five-gallon container onto the table surface.

Sink Installation

Step 5 - Using a plastic five-gallon container (R) (4.9-gallon, 10⅞" x 15⅞" actual size) as a guide, trace the 11" x 16" contour onto the upper table surface as shown in Step 5. Check the size of your container and make any adjustments necessary.

Dadoes

Step 6 - The front edge of the container should be flush with the back edge of the front-most slat, and the right side of the container should be 4⅛" in from the right edge of the slat ends. Remove the table slats and cut to size. Use a dado blade set to the proper height to cut the rear-most butted slat as shown in Step 6.

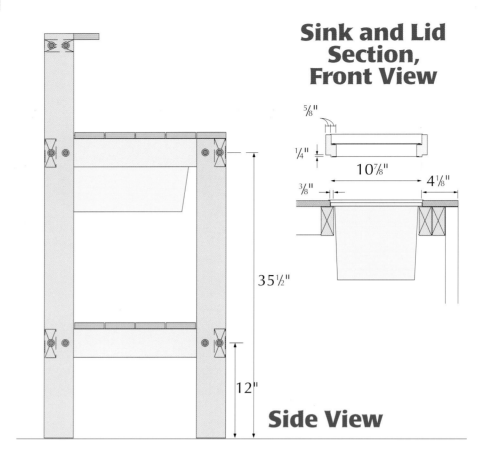

Sink and Lid Section, Front View

35½"

12"

Side View

10⅞"

4⅛"

⅝"

¼"

⅜"

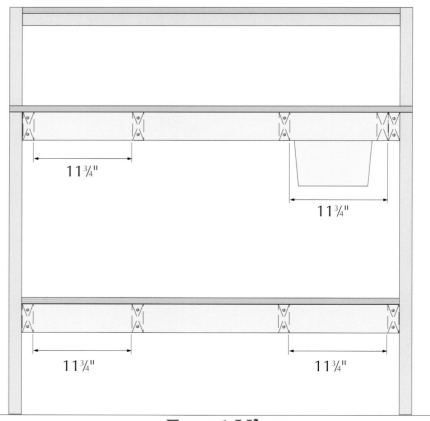

11¾"

11¾"

11¾"

11¾"

Front View

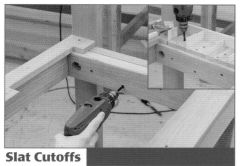

Slat Cutoffs

Step 7 - Reattach the rear-most slat and screw one of the stretchers left off earlier to the right-most stretcher as shown in Step 7. Be sure to pre-drill screw holes and cut holes to accommodate the bolts protruding from the adjacent stretcher. Pre-drill a second hole into each slat off-cut and reattach small slats using ⅛" spacers and a fence clamped along the right edge of the table as shown in the inset photo in Step 7. (Note that the ends of the slat offcuts should fall ⅜" shy of the stretcher edge to provide the right-side lip for the container, once inserted.)

Attach the remaining stretcher to the rails and screw down the table slats. (Again, there should be a ⅜" lip along the stretcher edge to hold the container in place, once inserted.)

Top Shelf

Step 8 - Position the remaining rail between the back legs using ¾"-thick scraps to hold the rail in place as shown in Step 8. Pre-drill into the endgrain of the rail for lag screws using the existing holes in each leg as guides. Screw the rail in place using washers and lag screws; then remove the scraps.

Cut the top shelf (G) to the dimensions given in the material list. Clamp the top shelf in place and drill pilot holes through the shelf and into the rail. Stagger the holes to avoid splitting along the grain and insert screws as shown in the inset photo in Step 8. Round the front corners of the shelf with sandpaper. Refer to exploded drawing for top shelf detail.

Sink Lid Ends

Step 9 - Cut the sink lid ends (H) and lid sides (I) to the dimensions given in the material list. Cut a through rabbet into the top inside edge of each lid side using a ⅜" dado head set to a depth of 1¼" on the table saw. Cut stopped rabbets ⅜" in from each end into the lid ends as shown in Step 9. Square off the stopped grooves on the router table or with a chisel. Pre-drill screw holes into each lid end and assemble the lid frame.

Rabbets

Step 10 - Reposition the fence on the table saw and run the lid bottom over the ⅜" dado head set to a depth of ¼" as shown in Step 10. (The resulting rabbet should measure ⅜" x ¼"-deep.) Repeat the dado cut on the opposite edge of the lid bottom; then reposition the fence to cut the same rabbet along the lid ends. Cut an 11" x 16" piece of ½" wire mesh and pre-drill at least six holes into the recessed groove on the top side of the lid. Screw down the mesh using ⅜" washers to keep the screen in place as shown in the inset photo in Step 10. Finish the entire table with an exterior water sealer, making sure all surfaces are coated thoroughly.

The removable sink feature allows you to use separate five-gallon containers for watering, transplanting and soil mixing. A ¼" lip, cut into the underside of the lid, keeps the tray secure while you go about your work. The lid above employs ½" wire mesh for maximum durability. Any size mesh or screen can be used, however, depending on your potting needs.

See Pattern Page 1 for full-size patterns.

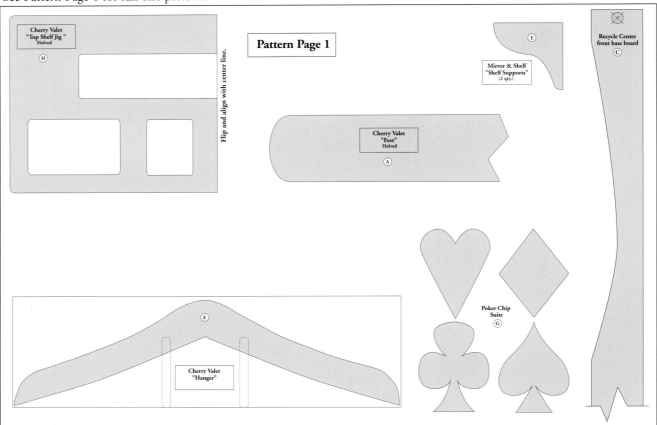

See Pattern Page 2 for full-size patterns.

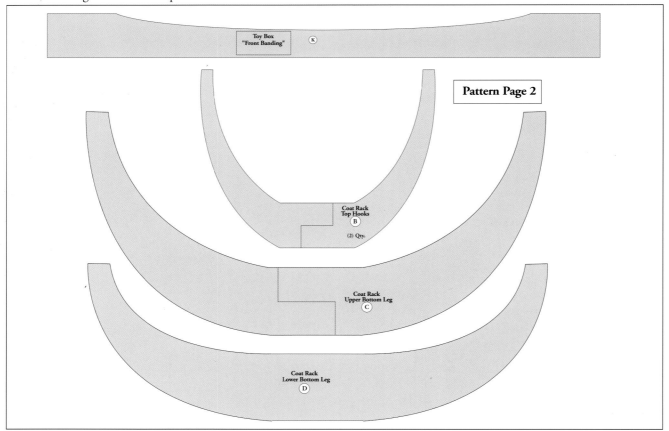

See Pattern Page 3 for full-size patterns.

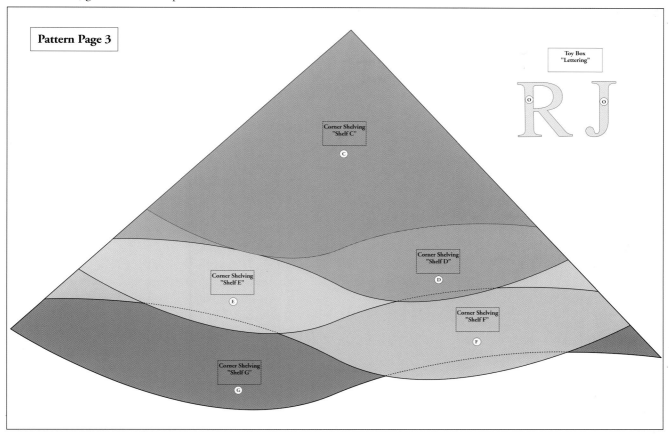

See Pattern Page 4 for full-size patterns.

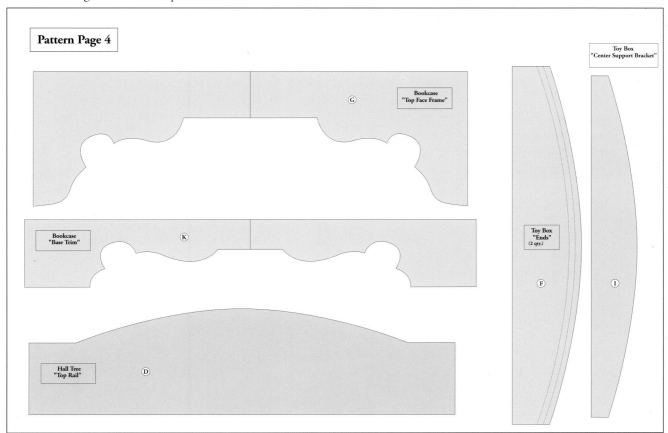

More Great Project Books from Fox Chapel Publishing

How-To Book of Birdhouses and Feeders
By Paul Meisel
This book features 30 birdhouse and feeder projects using common woodworking shop tools. Also includes information about attracting birds to your backyard.
ISBN: 1-56523-237-2, 208 pages, soft cover, $19.95

Intarsia Workbook
By Judy Gale Roberts and Jerry Booher
You'll be amazed at the beautiful pictures you can create when you learn to combine different colors and textures of wood to make raised, 3-D images. Features 7 projects and expert instruction. Great for beginners!
ISBN: 1-56523-226-7, 72 pages, soft cover, $14.95

Making Lawn Ornaments in Wood
By Paul Meisel
Stop traffic with these popular lawn and garden accessories. Features complete instructions and patterns for 34 projects, a full-color gallery and a paint mixing chart. Detailed instructions cover choosing the wood, transferring, cutting and painting.
ISBN: 1-56523- 163-5, 72 pages, soft cover, $14.95

Fireplace and Mantel Ideas, 2nd edition
By John Lewman
Design, build and install your dream fireplace mantel with this updated edition of a popular classic. You'll find step-by-step instructions for carving a rustic mantel and building a classic fireplace mantel, and an amazing selection of classic fireplace mantel designs like English traditional, Country French, Victorian, Art Nouveau, and more.
ISBN: 1-56523-229-1, 196 pages, soft cover, $19.95

Scroll Saw Workbook 2nd Edition
by John A. Nelson
The ultimate beginner's scrolling guide! Hone your scroll saw skills to perfection with the 25 skill-building chapters and projects included in this book. Techniques and patterns for wood and non-wood projects!
ISBN: 1-56523-207-0, 88 pages, soft cover, $14.95

Woodworking Projects for Women
By Linda Hendry
One of America's most accomplished woodworkers, Linda Hendry, guides other women step-by-step, through 15 Easy-to-Build Projects for the Home and Garden. The book is designed to build your confidence, and has full-color photographs and easy-to-follow instructions.
ISBN: 1-56523-247X, 72 pages, soft cover, $17.95

Make Your Own Model Dinosaur
By Danny A. Downs with Tom Knight
Everything you need to create exciting wooden dinosaur models–just like the ones in the museum stores! Inside you will find patterns and instructions for cutting and assembling seven different dinosaur projects. From the tyrannosaurus rex to the velociraptor, you'll find patterns for each and every dinosaur detail. Once all of the pieces are cut, share the fun with your friends and family.
ISBN: 1-56523-079-5, 112 pages, soft cover, $17.95

Making Doll Furniture in Wood
By Dennis Simmons
Learn to make hand-made doll furniture with the 30 projects featured in this book! Inside you will find 5 step-by-step projects for a bed, dresser, chair and more. You'll also find measured drawings for an additional 25 pieces of furniture. Projects are perfectly sized for American Girl® or any other 18" doll.
ISBN: 1-56523-200-3, 120 pages, soft cover, $19.95

Woodworker's Guide to Making Traditional Mirrors and Picture Frames
By John A. Nelson
A sourcebook of patterns for woodworkers that features plans for mirrors and frames. Learn the basics behind cutting wood for mirrors and frames, and then use the included measured drawings to create your own.
ISBN: 1-56523-223-2, 112 pages, soft cover, $17.95

CHECK WITH YOUR LOCAL BOOK OR WOODWORKING STORE
Or call 800-457-9112 • Visit www.FoxChapelPublishing.com